Dear Jessica,

Grammar toward Professionalism

by

Dr. Martha J.B. Cook

Martha J.B. Cook

I love tennis too; keep up the good work.

I won the 2005 senior olympics in tennis singles and doubles in Pittsburgh. God Bless You.

RoseDog 🐾 Books

PITTSBURGH, PENNSYLVANIA 15222

ISBN # 0-8059-9868-3
Printed in the United States of America

First Printing

For additional information or to order additional books,
please write:
RoseDog Publishing
701 Smithfield Street
Pittsburgh, Pennsylvania 15222
U.S.A.
1-800-834-1803
Or visit our web site and on-line bookstore at
www.rosedogbookstore.com

UNIQUE FEATURES OF THIS BOOK ARE:

1) the National Achieve Standards and the Ohio Department of Education Academic Content Standards K—12 English Language Arts—Grammar Punctuation, Capitalization etc. (Appendix A)

2) grade designation throughout the book to tell the user what is taught at each level (Appendix A)

3) the oganization based on Maslow's Hierarchy of needs (cover)

4) the design for any level of sophistication from preschool through graduate school to doctoral dissertations

5) the introduction which gives teachers, tutors, parents, grandparents, etc. excellent ideas of how to use the book effectively at any level

6) that the book is not meant to delve into the depths of grammar but is designed by example to help with the crucial elements of grammar; the examples (models) teach vocabulary across the curriculum

7) a test to diagnose the strengths and weakness of the user (appendix B)

8) vocabulary words based on standardized tests and on prefixes, suffixes and roots (Appendix C)

9) common foreign words most often found in English scripts and their meanings; this is invaluable because most readers just skip them or guess at their meanings (Appendix D)

10) Roman numerals which are "foreign" to some people; this book goes beyond counting to "C" (100)

11) making writing a pleasant experience if one first learns to parodize (I think I coined that word) from examples; this book contains original examples of genre using bibliotherapy, drama, essay, fiction (parable), non fiction (history), poetry etc. (Appendix E)

Don't overlook the experience of the author who has taught every level of English mentioned in this book and has researched what is needed and what works!

DEDICATION

It doesn't usually take an author forty-five years to write a book. That's how long it took to write this one!

I want to give long deserved praise to my seventh and eighth grade classes at East Sparta High School (1951-53) who collectively said to me, "I could learn grammar if I knew where to look for the answers." That started this book and its logical progression from the simple to the complex.

Over the years my son, Mark, who is an accomplished speaker, and my husband Marvin, who is an award winning dairy farmer, and in his own right an accomplished speaker, have shown me where the critical issues are in grammar and helped me explain them to the layperson.

The graduate workshops I have given to numerous teachers, pastors, business people, nurses and potential authors have added to the insight of this work.

The wonderful, dedicated work of tutors, who have helped and are helping young people in their struggles to read, comprehend, write and speak grammatically correct, need to be given their due credit. The most notable of these is my sister Thelma Barber Powell, who is still tutoring and she is past eighty-five! These people along with practicing classroom teachers have all fed me information to simplify, clarify, and organize the material in this book.

Without the help of my Savior, I would not have kept with this project. I prayed that He would guide me if He felt I had a project that would be worthy. I still ask Him to help me use this work in whatever way may benefit mankind.

December 2004

The clear expression of thought is best articulated by those who understand the essential elements of grammar. Used properly, grammar is the tool that creates effective communication. Like many others, I was fortunate to have a teacher who not only understood the value of language skills but was also able to successfully pass on their worth to her students.

Dr. Martha Cook instilled in me a lifelong appreciation for the importance of good communication skills. Thank goodness that in today's world of abbreviated e-mail and text-messaging there are still teachers like Dr. Cook willing and able to share their expertise and appreciation for language skills.

John Bankert
President, Pro Football Hall of Fame
Canton, Ohio

December 2004

I took Dr. Cook's English 120 course at Malone College in 2001 and during the year all students had to make a grammar book as she instructed. It was a tedious journey making the book; however, the book helped me immensely when writing papers for my other classes and is still of help three years later. The grammar book should be a keepsake.

Mattathias Johnson
Junior – Business Administration, Malone College
Canton, Ohio

December 2004

Martha Cook's Grammar Toward Professionalism is long overdue! Today's educators need quick and comprehensible reference so that they are better prepared to model, teach, and support correct grammar and usage among schoolchildren today who lack such preparation. As a pre-service teacher educator I see tremendous value in incorporating use of her book as a supportive text in the preparation of future educators. Kudos to Dr. Cook for her persistence and patience in preparing this valuable resource.

Beth Clark-Thomas, Ph.D.
Associate Professor of Education
Malone College, Canton Ohio

INTRODUCTION

This book comes as a result of over forty years struggling with the teaching of grammar. It is designed to be all things to all people at all levels. It is organized to be as flexible or as structured as the user wishes.

The overall organization begins with the smallest unit of writing(excluding morphemes)— the words. Each part of speech is broken into definition, kinds (where applicable) and uses. A formula adapted from chemistry is used to help students remember the kinds. This is sometimes called initial letter strategy. Examples are given to further help the user.

The book takes the user from words (bricks) to phrases to clauses to sentences (structure). This is a natural progression in building toward expression.

Punctuation, capitalization and spelling become the "mortar" to make the finished product useable. Spelling may be handled any way the user wishes. The basic spelling rules may or may not be taught. The emphasis for spelling is largely on structure such as prefixes, roots and suffixes.

A longer piece of writing should not be done without an outline. Any oral presentation should also have an outline. The basics of organization and the different kinds of outlines for different audiences are presented. Stress is placed on the use of a Thesaurus.

Editing, proofing or simply finding one's mistakes is essential to the finished product. This section may be as personalized as the user wishes.

A glossary or definition of terms is essential since the English language may have multiple names for the same structure.

The text should be a loose-leaf notebook so that pages may be inserted at the discretion of the user.

Examples throughout the text should be made to upgrade vocabulary. Example: Cats are felines; kangaroos are marsupials.

The text should be copied from a chalkboard, overhead projector or computer depending on the availability or lack of technology. The notes should be copied in the class if this text is used in the classroom. This is necessary to add other dimensions to language use—reading, copying, understanding, transcribing, and using. This is essential for placing the reference whereabouts into the long-term memory. This is based on the theory that if you don't have the actual facts in your long term memory, at least know where to find them in this reference book in your long term memory. This is a tremendous time-saving device for the teacher evaluating compositions. Simply refer to the page or section of the text that <u>they wrote</u> to learn why the mistake was made and how it may be corrected.

Effort has been made throughout the text to coordinate all content areas into this book – chemistry formulae, mathematical ratios, physical education parallels, foreign language links, business abbreviations, historical research, and flexibility to add, change, or modify any section.

This text may be color coded so that each level of instruction builds on the former. The succeeding level knows what has been taught at the preceding level.

This text is designed to accompany any student to his next educational experience be it at the same school or a new school. It is also designed so that the teacher may copy the text to the point of entry for a new student entering the school.

Make up work is facilitated mostly through cooperative learning. A "buddy" or mentor helps in the make-up phase when necessary.

This text becomes a portfolio for use beyond the classroom. It is designed for secretaries, ministers, tutors, grandparents, everyone.

The climaxing beauty of the process is that the user writes his own text, puts a creative cover on it, learns to read, copy, spell, correct, reference, use and reuse.

Now grammar isn't so bad after all. <u>You have written a book.</u>

TABLE OF CONTENTS

Complex
Compound-complex
Uses
Declarative
Interrogative
Imperative
Exclamatory

Period
Comma
Colon
Semi-colon
Question mark
Exclamation mark
Quotation marks (Direct and Indirect)
Parentheses
Dash
Brackets
Apostrophe
Hyphen
Underlining or Italicization
Virgule (slash)
Caret

Proper nouns
Sentences
Poetry
Quotations
Directions
Single letter words

Prefixes
Suffixes
Roots
Roman Numerals

ACKNOWLEDGMENTS

To the President of Malone College in Canton, Ohio, Dr. Ron Johnson, and the Board of Trustees who made this book become a fruition by granting me a sabbatical: Wayne Blizzard, Pamela Burch, Dale Chryst, Sally Efremoff, Wayne Ickes, William Lockwood, Roger Mann, Keith Martig, Nancy McPeek, Paul Miller, Edward Mitchell, David Murray, Richard Pittenger, James Powell, David Rawson, Frank Raymond, Carol Reed, Willis Ruff, Dena Schnupp, Gerald Smeltzer, Sandra Stark, Steven Steer, Phillip Teague, John Williams, Jr., Michael Zetz.

To the people who helped me with the technical parts of this book I am grateful and learned how much work it takes to put a book together using a computer; namely, David Snyder, Tom Love, Diane and Fred Merritt, Pastor Jack Wingate, Mike Farber.

To the third and fourth grade teachers at Waynesburg Elementary School in the Sandy Valley School District, Waynesburg, Ohio who graciously supplied me with the vocabulary words which appear throughout the book to help students with the vocabulary found in some proficiency tests.

To the Education Faculty members of Malone College who critiqued my book: David Bowman, Maxine Burgett, Beth Clark-Thomas, Paul Davidson, Tom Grove, Marshall Holmes, Mark Jakowski, Christine Krol, Patricia Long, Donald Williams.

To the Departments of Visual Arts Education: Anne Coen, Barbara Drennan, Clare Murray, J. Willis; Social Work: Jane Hoyt-Oliver, Ken Stoltzfus; Natural Science: Bob Moffitt, William McVaugh, Donghai Chen, Christopher Carmichael, Jeff Goff, Steve Diakoff; Health and Human Performance: Barbara Easlick, Kathy Haas, Ken Hoalt, Pam Hoalt, Jack Hazen, Charles Grimes, Hal Smith, Lori Wynn; Nursing: Margaret Halter, Martha Horst, Jennifer Hostutler, Linda Leon, Christy Pester, Stephanie

Reagan, Loretta Reinhart, Elizabeth Rettew, Susan Taylor, Robin Tomin, Lora Wyss; Fine Arts music: Jack Ballard, Sandra Carnes, Jerry Giger, Rachel Nunez, Jonathan Willis; Business: Tom Kratzer, John Harris, Julia Sampson, Dennis Kincaid, Michael Ophardt, Roy Ramsaroop, Albert Smith, Julie Szendrey; Foreign Language: Julia Villasenor. These people all gave me audience to present my pleas that grammar is something that all educators must help to improve among their students and they gave me essential ideas to make this book a tool to accomplish this.

To the graduate class in marketing taught by Maria Lam and especially Mark Rhinehart, Jacqui Schmotzer and Sandy Kocher who surveyed and statistically calculated the essential part of this book to make it marketable.

A special *kudos* to Cara Gabriel whose art work "dressed up" my book and whose help in organization made my book even more palatable to the reader.

To my parents who taught me that God gave me intelligence, strength, patience, and desire and all my life I should be a "long distance runner" (Appendix E) and then leave a legacy to posterity. This is my legacy.

Chapter I

EIGHT PARTS OF
SPEECH BY
FAMILIES

- FAMILY ONE –
  NOUNS,
  PRONOUNS,
  ADJECTIVES

- FAMILY TWO--
  VERBS,ADVERBS

- FAMILY THREE –
  CONJUNCTIONS,
  PREPOSITIONS

- FAMILY FOUR –
  THE MAVERICK –
  INTERJECTIONS

CHAPTER I

Eight Parts of Speech
Noun, Pronoun, Adjective (family number one)
Verb, Adverb (family number two)
Preposition, Conjunction (family number three)
Interjection (maverick)

NOUNS (4 kinds)

Definition: A noun is a part of speech which names a person (Martha), an object (book), an event(game),or a thing (honesty). *ONE**

Kinds: C₂ A P (a formula to help remember kinds; initial letter strategy)

1. <u>Common</u>: the name of any person (boy), place (playground) or thing (car). *ONE*

2. <u>Collective</u>: the name of a whole group or collection of persons or things used as one entity (herd). *SIX*
   Note: Most collective nouns are singular.

3. <u>Abstract</u>: the name of a quality or general characteristic of a thing (redness, honesty, beauty, love).*SIX*

4. <u>Proper</u>: the name of a particular person (William McKinley),or place (Ohio). *ONE*
   Note: A proper noun is always capitalized.

*BOLD ITALICS MARK THE LEVEL EACH SHOULD BE TAUGHT ACCORDING TO OHIO DEPT. OF EDUCATION ACADEMIC STANDARDS K—12 ENGLISH LANGUAGE ARTS APPENDIX A

Uses:

SUBJECTIVE CASE (3 uses) *FOUR*

1. subject of a sentence
   Example: <u>Kangaroos</u> are marsupials.

2. predicate noun of a sentence
   A predicate noun will always follow a copulative (linking) verb and be the same person or thing as the subject.
   Example: An opossum is a <u>marsupial.</u>

3. direct address: naming the person to whom you are speaking
   Example: <u>Martha</u>, will you come here?
   (sometimes called vocative case instead of subjective case}

OBJECTIVE CASE (4 USES) *FOUR*

1. indirect object of a sentence
   Example: Mother baked <u>Bobby</u> a cake.

   Note: An indirect object will always be followed by a direct object and will answer the question whom or what about the direct object.

2. direct object of a sentence
   Example: Mother baked Bobby a <u>cake</u>.
   Note: A direct object will always follow the indirect object and answer the question whom or what about the verb.

3. object of a preposition
   Example: Mother baked a cake (for the <u>boy</u>).
   Note: A prepositional phrase will begin with a preposition and end with its object a noun or pronoun in the objective case. The object of a preposition will always be the last word of a prepositional phrase.

4. <u>subject</u> and <u>object</u> of an (infinitive) *FOUR*
   Example: He wanted the <u>dog</u> (to eat)the <u>meat</u>.
   Note: An infinitive is "to" plus a verb.

SUBJECTIVE OR OBJECTIVE CASE *FOUR*

1. A noun may be used in apposition
   Example: <u>Bill,</u> the <u>salesman,</u> drives a red car. (subjective case)

4

Example: A red car was driven by <u>Bill</u>, the <u>salesman</u>.
(objective case)

Note: The appositive is always the same case as the word in which it is in apposition.

POSSESSIVE CASE *THREE*

1. To make a noun singular possessive, write the word in its singular form and then add an apostrophe and an s.
    Example: (girl's)

2. Sometimes singular nouns already end in an s. When this happens, just add an apostrophe.
    Example:(Doris')

1. To make a noun plural possessive write the word in its plural form and just add an apostrophe.
    Example: boxes'

2. Sometimes plural words do not end in an s, so add an apostrophe and an s.
    Example: women's men's (These are called irregular plural nouns).*THREE*

Note: Pronouns have the same uses (cases) as nouns because a pronoun is a substitute for a noun.

PRONOUNS (8 kinds)

Definition: A pronoun is a part of speech which takes the place of   (substitutes for) a noun. *THREE*

Kinds: D R₃ I₂ P₂ (a formula which helps remember the kinds)

1. <u>Demonstrative</u>   *NINE—TWELVE*
    Singular   Plural
    this   these
    that   those

Example: <u>This</u> is my book. <u>These</u> are my books.

2. <u>Reciprocal</u>   ***NINE—TWELVE***
   each other   one another
   Example: They hurt <u>each other</u>.

3. <u>Reflexive</u>   ***NINE—TWELVE***
   myself, yourself
   Examples: I hurt <u>myself</u>.
   They hurt <u>themselves</u>.
   Note: will end in self or selves

   3a. Intensive—I, myself, will go. ***NINE—TWELVE***
       (another use for reflexive)

4. <u>Relative</u> - connects the dependent (or subordinate) clause with the independent (principal, main) clause ***FIVE***
   Who, whose, whom refers to persons or named animals (Bambi). Which, what refers to unnamed animals (tiger) or things (box). That refers to persons, animals, or things.
   Example: He is the boy <u>who</u> consumed (ate) two pizzas.

5. <u>Indefinite</u> - does not clearly point out any particular person, place or thing. ***FIVE***
   (each, some, any, either, neither, one, all, both, someone, anyone, no one, none, everyone, nobody, somebody, few, others)
   Example: <u>Each</u> is carrying his own lunch.
   Note: indefinite pronouns are usually singular in number

6. <u>Interrogative</u> - always asks a question ***FOUR***
   (who, what, which, whose)
   Example: <u>Who</u> called me?

*7. <u>Possessive</u> - denotes ownership or possession ***THREE***
    (see table on next page)

8. <u>Personal</u> - First person is speaker (I, me). ***THREE*
    Second person is spoken to (you).
    Third person is spoken about
    (she, he, it, they).
    (see table on next page)

*third column below **first and second columns below

PRONOUNS (table)

Column I *THREE*	Column II *THREE*	Column III *THREE*
Singular	Singular	Singular
**Personal	**Personal	*Possessive
Subjective Case	Objective Case	Case
I	Me	Mine
You	You	Yours
She (feminine)	Her	Hers
He (masculine)	Him	His
It (neuter)	It	Its

Plural Personal		Plural
Subjective	Objective	Possessive
Case	Case	Case
We	Us	Ours
You	You	Yours
They	Them	Theirs

CAVEAT (beware): When a pronoun is the object of a preposition, it must be in the objective case.(Column II above)

CAVEAT: When a pronoun follows a copulative (linking) verb, it is called a predicate pronoun and is in the subjective case (Column I above)

Note: Personal pronouns have person such as:

I and We are called first person and are the persons speaking.
You is called second person and is the person spoken about. **"You" will always take a plural verb.**
She, He, It and They are called third person and are the persons spoken to. **In the singular there is gender indication.**

These **relative** pronouns have case. *FIVE*

Subjective	Objective	Possessive
Who	Whom	Whose

Note: PRONOUNS HAVE THE SAME USES AND CASES AS

NOUNS. This is one of the most prevalent errors both writers and speakers make. Every time you want to use a pronoun, go back to the noun for which it stands (antecedent) and make them both either singular or plural; this is called agreement. ***THREE***

CAVEAT: A PRONOUN MUST AGREE IN NUMBER (SINGULAR OR PLURAL) AND GENDER (MASCULINE, FEMININE OR NEUTER) WITH THE NOUN (ANTECEDENT) FOR WHICH THE PRONOUN STANDS. ***THREE***

ADJECTIVES(7)

Definition: An adjective is a part of speech which describes or modifies a noun or pronoun. ***TWO***

Kinds: D_2 R I_2 P N (a formula to help remember kinds)

1. Descriptive - describes a noun. ***ONE***
    Example: He entertained a <u>large</u> group.

2. Demonstrative - demonstrates or points out. ***NINE—TWELVE***
    This, that are singular.
    Example: <u>This</u> book is mine.
    These, those are plural.
    Example: <u>These</u> books are mine.

3. Relative - Relates. ***FIVE***
    Which, whichever, what, whatever
    Example: He always does <u>whatever</u> work he promises.

4. Indefinite- does not clearly point out any particular person, place or thing. **FIVE**
    (any, all, another, every, each, either, neither, few, many, numerous, other, one, none, some, several, such, various—a and an are called indefinite article adjectives)
    Example: <u>Each</u> person here has had the flu.
    Example: <u>The</u> Ohio State University is large.

Note: There is only one definite article adjective and that is the word "the."

Note: To make some indefinite adjectives possessive add an apostrophe.

8

(One's, one another's, each other's are indefinite adjectives but *FIVE* always contain an apostrophe when used possessively).
Example: <u>One's</u> team should be well coached.

5. <u>Interrogative</u> - always begins a question. *THREE*
    (what, which, whose)
    Example: <u>What</u> game are you playing? (singular)
    Example: <u>Which</u> animal has a long trunk?
    Example: <u>Whose</u> scarves are those? (plural)

6. <u>Possessive</u> - denotes ownership or possession of a noun. *THREE*

		Singular	Plural
First Person		my (book)	our (books)
Second Person		your	your
Third Person			their
	feminine	her	
	masculine	his	
	neuter	its	

Example: <u>His</u> hat was stolen. <u>Their</u> hats were stolen.

Note: An adjective will nearly always be followed by a noun or pronoun. Some grammar texts do not distinguish between a possessive pronoun and a possessive adjective.

7. <u>Numerical</u> - denotes quantity such as one, two, three etc. *EIGHT*
    -denotes order such as first, second etc.
    Example: The sum (adding numbers) of <u>two</u> boys and four boys is <u>six</u> boys.
    Example: The <u>second</u> row may go to the drinking fountain.

. . . .

Nearly all adjectives (and adverbs) have three degrees of comparison called:

1. Positive - only one item is involved. *SIX*
    Example: The computer is a <u>good</u> resource (means of finding information).

2. Comparative - two items are involved. *SIX*
    Example: An encyclopedia may be a <u>better</u> resource of finding information than a computer.

9

3. Superlative - three or more items are involved. *SIX*
   Example: The <u>best</u> source of gaining information is to listen and understand expert teachers.

   On two syllable adjectives use "er" for the comparative and "est" for the superlative (tall, taller, tallest).

   On three syllable adjectives use "more" for comparative and "most" for superlative (dangerous, more dangerous, most dangerous). *SIX*

Note: When comparing one person with members of a group, use "else" or "other" with the comparative. *NINE—TWELVE*

   Example: Ann is taller (predicate adjective) than anyone else in her family.

Note: When comparing one person with members of a group, use "all" with the superlative. *NINE—TWELVE*
   Example: Joe is the <u>tallest</u> of all his ancestors (grandparents, great grandparents, et cetera).

VERBS (3 kinds)

Definition: a verb is a part of speech that shows action, tells what the subject does or shows position or state of being. *ONE*

Kinds: A₂ L (a formula to remember the kinds)

1. <u>Action</u> – shows activity *ONE*

2. <u>Auxiliary</u> (helping) - all verbs in a verb phrase except the very last verb will be auxiliary or linking (can, be, do, have, had, shall etc. *FOUR*
   Example: I <u>can </u>write well.

3. <u>Linking</u> or sometimes called copulative-(position) *FOUR*

   **Memorize this list of copulative (linking) verbs.
   (be, am, is, are, was, were, seem, grow, become, appear, the five

senses [feel, taste, smell, sound, look], all forms of been such as might have been, could have been, should have been, et cetera). Example: This is <u>she</u> speaking.

CAVEAT: If a noun or pronoun follows a copulative (linking) verb in a sentence and is the same person or thing as the subject, the noun or pronoun must be in the subjective (nominative) case. (see subjective case under nouns and pronouns)

Principal parts: (Most verbs have four). **FOUR**

Present principal part	go
Past principal part	went
Present participle principal part	going
Past participle principal part	gone

Tenses = Time *FOUR*

The six regular tenses used to signify time in sentences.

			Principal part used to make the tenses
1.	Present	I work	Present principal part *THREE*
2.	Past	I worked.	Past principal part *THREE*
3.	Future	I shall work.	Present principal part with auxiliary (shall or will) *THREE*
4.	Present Perfect	I have worked.	Past participle principal part with auxiliary (have, has) *SIX*
5.	Past Perfect	I had worked	Past participle principal part with auxiliary (had) *SIX*
6.	Future Perfect	I shall have worked.	Past participle principal part with auxiliary (shall or will) *SIX*

Note: The progressive tenses have some form of the verb "be" plus the present participle. *EIGHT*

Example: I am working.

WHEN TO USE THE TENSES *NINE—TWELVE*

Present – action now going on or recently stopped

Example: Right now I <u>observe</u> (look at) the rules of grammar.
Past - action ended sometime ago.
Example: Last month I <u>observed</u> the rules of grammar and I learned them.

Future - action has not yet occurred.
Example: In my next composition I <u>shall observe</u> the rules because I shall review them.

Present perfect - action to the present but may not continue
Example: I <u>have observed</u> the rules but I may not next time if I forget.
Past perfect - action ended before another action began
Example: I <u>had observed</u> the rules before I lost my grammar book.

Future perfect - future action which will end before another future action begins.
Example: I <u>shall have observed</u> the rules until I get too nervous or careless

. . . .

Note: When the third and fourth principal parts are not used as verbs, they may be a participle (verbal) and will be followed by a noun or pronoun. *EIGHT*

Note: The third principal part may be used as a noun and it is called a gerund. *EIGHT*

CAVEAT: Make every verb agree in number (singular or plural) with the subject. (See subjunctive mood [p. 13] for exception)

Note: Two or more singular subjects joined by 'or' or 'nor' take a singular verb but if one subject is singular and one subject plural, the verb agrees with the nearer.
Example: Martha or Alan is going. (singular)
Example: Martha or her children are going.(plural)*NINE—TWELVE*

Note: A singular verb will usually end in an 's' and a plural verb will not.

Moods: most verbs can be written in three moods. *EIGHT*
1. <u>Indicative</u> – is a statement of fact.
   Example: I am happy. (We speak in this most often).

2. <u>Subjunctive</u> – is to put a condition in writing. *EIGHT*
   Example: If I were an archaeologist, I would study dead things.
CAVEAT: In subjunctive mood a plural verb is used with a singular subject.

3. <u>Imperative</u>: is a command. The subject is an ellipsis. *EIGHT*
   Example: (You) Shut the door! (You) is called an ellipsis; it is understood but not said or written.

Voice: Most verbs can be written in two voices. *NINE—TWELVE*

1. <u>Active</u>:
   Example; I write fiction (untrue stories).The subject (I) does what the verb (write) says.
2. <u>Passive</u>: Use a form of the verb "be" plus the past participle.
   Example: Fiction is written by me. Passive voice is weaker; use sparingly.

Note: To change to passive—take the subject out (I), put the direct object in (ball), change the verb to a verb phrase using some form of "be" then put the former subject as the object of the prepositional phrase (me).

<u>Transitive</u>: All transitive verbs have direct objects. *SIX*
Example: Bob used a compass (a direction finder [North, East, West, South]) to find his way.
Subject + verb + direct object

<u>Intransitive</u>: Intransitive verbs do **not** have direct objects. *SIX*
All copulative (linking) verbs are intransitive.
Examples: Bob is an entrepreneur (business manager).

Note: No intransitive verb can be passive.

. . . .

Verbals: *CAVEAT* (THESE ARE NOT VERBS) *EIGHT*

<u>Gerund</u> is 1/2 verb(looks) plus 1/2 noun(use). *EIGHT*

Example: <u>Comparing</u> is how things are alike.
Note: a gerund will always end in "ing."
Hint: The "n" in gerund stands for noun.

<u>Participle</u> is 1/2 verb(looks)plus 1/2 adjective(use). *EIGHT*
Present participle:
Example: <u>Comparing people </u>(how they are alike) sometimes hurts
their feelings.

Note: A present participle will always end in "ing."
Hint: The "a" in participle stands for adjective.

Past participle: *EIGHT*
Example: The <u>contrasted</u> (how they are different) <u>couple</u> are frater-
nal twins.

Note: A past participle will end in any way that a fourth column verb
ends.(see pages 15, 16, 17)

<u>Infinitive</u> is "to + a verb." An infinitive can function as a noun, adjec-
tive, or adverb. *EIGHT*
Example: <u>To predict</u> is to tell what you think will happen (noun).

Note: Use only columns I and IV for infinitives (see pages 15, 16, 17 with
columns of verbs) Infinitives can only be present and present perfect tenses.

SOME COMMON IRREGULAR VERBS
AND THEIR USES AS *VERBALS

I	II	III	IV
PRESENT	PAST	PROGRESSIVE	PAST PARTICIPLE
PRINCIPAL	PRINCIPAL	TENSE	PRINCIPAL
PART	PART	*SIX*	PART
FOUR	*FOUR*		*FOUR*
		*PRESENT *FOUR**	*PAST *FOUR**
		PARTICIPLE (adj.)	PARTICIPLE (adj.)
*INFINITIVE		*GERUND (noun)	*INFINITIVE
EIGHT		*EIGHT*	*EIGHT*

14

I	II	III	IV
arise	arose	arising	arisen
be,am,is,are	was,were	being	been
bear	bore	bearing	borne,born
beat	beat	beating	beaten
become	became	becoming	become
begin	began	beginning	begun
bite	bit	biting	bitten,bit
blow	blew	blowing	blown
break	broke	breaking	broken
bring	brought	bringing	brought
build	built	building	built
burst	burst	bursting	burst
buy	bought	buying	bought
choose	chose	choosing	chosen
come	came	coming	come
dig	dug	digging	dug
dive	dived,dove	diving	dived
do	did	doing	done
draw	drew	drawing	drawn
dream	dreamed,dreamt	dreaming	dreamed,dreamt
drink	drank	drinking	drunk
drive	drove	driving	driven
eat	ate	eating	eaten
fall	fell	falling	fallen
feel	felt	feeling	felt
fight	fought	fighting	fought
find	found	finding	found
fly	flew	flying	flown
forget	forgot	forgetting	forgotten,forgot
freeze	froze	freezing	frozen
get	got	getting	gotten,got
give	gave	giving	given
go	went	going	gone
grow	grew	growing	grown
hang(suspend)	hung	hanging	hung
hang(person)	hanged	hanging	hanged
have	had	having	had
hear	heard	hearing	heard

Note: Columns III and IV will always have an auxiliary verb used with it.

I	II	III	IV
hide	hid	hiding	hidden
keep	kept	keeping	kept
know	knew	knowing	known
lay	laid	laying	laid (has direct object)
lead	led	leading	led
leave	left	leaving	left
lend	lent	lending	lent
lie	lay	laying	lain (no direct object
lose	lost	losing	lost
make	made	making	made
mean	meant	meaning	meant
meet	met	meeting	met
ought	has only a present principal part		
pay	paid	paying	paid
prove	proved	proving	proved, proven
read	read	reading	read
ride	rode	riding	ridden
rang	rung	ringing	run
rise	rose	rising	rise
run	ran	running	run
say	said	saying	said
see	saw	seeing	seen
send	sent	sending	sent
set	set	setting	set (has a direct object
shake	shook	shaking	shaken
shoot	shot	shooting	shot
show	showed	showing	showed, shown
shrink	shrank	shrinking	shrunk
sing	sang	singing	sung
sink	sank	sinking	sunk
sit	sat	sitting	sat (has no direct object)
sleep	slept	sleeping	slept
speak	spoke	speaking	spoken
spend	spent	spending	spent
spring	sprang, sprung	springing	sprung
stand	stood	standing	stood

I	II	III	IV
steal	stole	stealing	stolen
strike	struck	striking	struck, stricken
swim	swam	swimming	swum
swing	swung	swinging	swung
take	took	taking	taken
teach	taught	teaching	taught
tear	tore	tearing	torn
tell	told	telling	told
think	thought	thinking	thought
throw	threw	throwing	thrown
wake	woke	waking	waked, woken
wear	wore	wearing	worn
win	won	winning	won
wind	wound	winding	wound
write	wrote	writing	written

CONJUGATION IN THE INDICATIVE MOOD OF THE MOST IRREGULAR VERB IN THE ENGLISH LANGUAGE (BE) *SEVEN*

Note: This is a pattern for conjugating all verbs.

Principal parts: **be, am, is, are** (Present Tense); **was, were**, (Past Tense); **being**, (Present Participle/Progressive Tense); past participle **been** (Present Perfect, Past Perfect, Future Perfect Tenses)

INDICATIVE MOOD (simple tenses)

	Singular Present Tense	Singular Past Tense	Singular Future Tense *THREE*
1st Person	I am	I was	I shall be
2nd	You are	You **were**	You will be
3rd	He is	He was	He will be
	She is	She was	She will be
	It is	It was	It will be
	Plural	Plural	Plural
	We are	We were	We shall be
	You are	You were	You will be
	They are	They were	They will be

INDICATIVE MOOD (perfect tenses) *SEVEN*

Singular	Singular	Singular
Present Perfect	Past Perfect	Future Perfect
Tense	Tense	Tense
I have been	I had been	I shall have been
You have been	You had been	You will have been
He **has** been	He had been	He will have been
She **has** been	She had been	She will have been
It **has** been	It had been	It will have been
Plural	Plural	Plural
We have been	We had been	We shall have been
You have been	You had been	You will have been
They have been	They had been	They will have been

CAVEAT: If shall and will are reversed in the future tense, the reader should read it as though it was a command!

SIMPLE PROGRESSIVE TENSES *SEVEN*
(Some form of auxiliary verb be with present participle)

I am being	I was being	I shall be being

PERFECT PROGRESSIVE TENSES **SEVEN**
I have been being I had been being I shall have been being

Note: See page on subjunctive and imperative moods.

Note: See page "when to use the tenses" in writing and speaking.

ADVERBS (5)

Definition: An adverb is a part of speech that modifies a verb, an adjective or another adverb. *FOUR*

Ad - <u>adjective</u>
Verb - ad<u>verb</u>
Adverb – <u>adverb</u>

(notice how the word "adverb" contains what it modifies)
Kinds: (5)

18

1. <u>Time:</u>   (when)   The sun shone <u>today.</u>
2. <u>Place:</u>   (where)   Meet me <u>there.</u>
3. <u>Manner:</u>   (how)   He behaved <u>badly.</u>
4. <u>Number:</u>   (how many times)   He hit me <u>twice.</u>
5. <u>Degree:</u>   (to what extent)   The sun shone <u>brightly.</u>

Note: Notice how knowing adverbs will help you in writing a news article for a newspaper.

• •

Degrees of comparison of adverbs (see also adjectives) *SIX*

1. Positive – only one item is involved.
   Example: The <u>dog</u> bites **ferociously**.

2. Comparative – two items are involved.
   Example: The <u>dog</u> bites **more ferociously** than the <u>cat.</u>

3. Superlative – three or more items are involved.
   Example: The <u>lions</u> bite the **most ferociously** of <u>all the cats.</u>

Note: When comparing members of a group, use "else" or "other" with the comparative and "all" with the superlative.*NINE—TWELVE*
   Examples:
   She is **farther** down the street than anyone else on the list.
   She is the **farthest** away of all members of the group.

Note: Use more and most with longer words. *SIX*
   Note: "Too," "there," and "here" are always adverbs.
   Example: There are **too** many people **here.**

Note: Negative words are adverbs.
   Example: She has **never** been to my home.

PREPOSITIONS

Definition: A preposition is a part of speech that shows relationship between the noun or pronoun that it takes as an object and some other word in the sentence. *FOUR*
Note: A preposition will always be used in a prepositional phrase

19

as the first word.
Example: He drove (**around** the block).

Common prepositions are:

aboard	between	on
above	but(except)	outside
across	by	over
after	down	regarding
along	during	throughout
amid	except(but)	to
among	for	toward
around	from	under
at	in	until
before	inside	up
behind	into	upon
beneath	of	with
beside	off	within (out)

Phrasal Prepositions may be more than one word but used as one part of speech.

according to	by way of	in spite of
along with	due to	instead of
apart from	except for	on account of
as far as	in addition to	out of
as for	in case of	up to
as regards	in front of	with regard to
as to	in lieu of	with respect to
because of	in place of	with reference to
by means of	in regard to	with the exception of
by reason of		

CAVEAT: (beware) The object of a preposition will never be the subject of a sentence.

Note: The object of a preposition will always be a noun or pronoun in the objective case.

CONJUNCTIONS (3) *THREE*

Definition: A conjunction is a part of speech that connects words, phrases or clauses. ***THREE***

Kinds: (3)

1. <u>Coordinate</u> conjunctions - connect words, phrases, clauses of the same rank or kind. (and, but, or, nor) ***THREE***
   Example: He **and** I are going.(words)
   Example: He went up the stairs **and** into the room.(phrases)
   Example: He ran **but** he fell. (clauses)
2. <u>Correlative</u> conjunctions - must be used in pairs. ***NINE—TWELVE***
   (either . . . or, neither . . . nor, not only . . . but also, whether . . . or)
   Example: You must **either** use good grammar **or** be judged as un-educated.

3. <u>Subordinate</u> conjunctions - connect a dependent (subordinate) clause with an independent (principal or main clause) ***SEVEN***

although	because	since	unless
after	before	than	when
as	for	that	where
as if	if	therefore	whether
as soon as	in order that	though	while

Example: (**Since** you are my friend), I will let you in.

Note: All subordinate clauses at the beginning of a sentence (beginning with a subordinate conjunction or a relative pronoun) are followed by a comma. ***NINE—TWELVE***

• •

INTERJECTIONS *FOUR*

Definition: An interjection is a part of speech that shows strong or sudden feeling.

ah	ha	oh
listen	boo	hey
alas	hurrah	yo (colloquial)
bang	ouch	

Example: **Ah**, now I see it.
Example: **Ouch**! You hit me.
Example: **Help**!

Note: Many profane words are interjections; do not use profanity because profanity is the result of a limited vocabulary.

Misplaced (dangling) Modifiers *EIGHT*

Modifiers should be placed as close as possible to the words they modify. Modifiers which are not positioned close to what they modify are called misplaced or dangling modifiers. They can lead to awkward, and in some instances, erroneous reading of the sentence. Some experimentation with placement of the word "only" in the following sentences will show how crucial the position of a single word can be to the meaning of a statement.

Examples:
Only we know of the man who invented the alphabet.

We only know of the man who invented the alphabet.

We know only of the man who invented the alphabet.

Note: Sometimes misplaced modifiers may be very embarrassing.

Example: Material was bought by a woman a yard wide.

Parallel Construction *EIGHT*

Parallel construction is one of the most efficient techniques in writing; it is necessary that you learn to write by paralleling your construction and it is not hard to learn.

Definition: Parallel structure means that two or more ideas in a sentence are expressed in similar form. Using the conjunctions "and," and "or," usually join like terms—two nouns, two adjectives, two verbs, two adverbs, two phrases, two clauses etc.

The following models will help you to understand how to write the correct structure in parallelism.

1.   *(Caveat)* Ruth likes painting and to read. Notice that (painting) is a gerund and (to read) is an infinitive.
1.   Ruth likes painting and reading or Ruth likes to paint and to read.

2.   *(Caveat)* He is handsome, intelligent, and has charm.
2.   He is handsome, intelligent and charming.

3.   *(Caveat)* We will get some things for cash but the rest on the payment of specified amounts at certain times.
3.   We will get some things for cash, but the rest on credit.

Note: Here we have the use of two prepositional phrases—(for cash) and (on credit).

Note: See how parallelism shortened the sentence.

Chapter II

**Putting it together
with finesse**

- **PHRASES**

- **CLAUSES**

- **SENTENCES**

Chapter II

PHRASES, CLAUSES, SENTENCES

PHRASES

Definition: A phrase is a group of related words but does not have a subject or predicate. *FOUR*

CAVEAT: A phrase cannot stand by itself as a sentence.

Kinds:
> Prepositional Phrase: *FOUR*

Note: All prepositions must have objects which must be a noun or pronoun. A preposition, a modifier of the noun or pronoun and the noun or pronoun usually make up a prepositional phrase.

Note: The entire prepositional phrase may be used as an adjective or an adverb.

Prepositional phrase used as an adjective. *NINE—TWELVE*
Example: It was an **in the mood** song.

Prepositional phrase used as an adverb. *NINE—TWELVE*
Example: He ran **around the house**.
> Verb Phrase: must be composed of at least two verbs (see section in Chapter I on auxiliary verbs) *THREE*

> Verbal phrases:(see section in Chapter I on verbals) *NINE—TWELVE*
>> Infinitive Phrase: (May be used as a noun, adjective, or adverb)
>> Example: **To skate** is fun. (noun, subject)

Example: Her plan was **to meet** us. (predicate adjective)
Example: Here lies a book **to read**. (adjective)
Example: He worked **to segregate** (separate) the mob. (adverb)

Gerundive Phrase:
(May be used any way a noun is used)
Example: **Spelling each word** is easy. (subject)
Example: His hobby is **the art of spelling**. (predicate noun)
Example: She is good in **the art of spelling**. (object of preposition)
Example: Jessie expects to learn **the art of spelling**. (object of an infinitive)

Participial Phrase:
(May be used any way an adjective is used)
Example: The dog **eating the bone** is mine. (sometimes called an adjective phrase)

CLAUSES (2) *SEVEN*

Definition: A clause is a part of a sentence and must contain a subject and a predicate. Either may be an ellipsis.

Kinds:
1. Principal (main or independent) clause expresses a complete thought when used by itself.
   Example: When it rains, **the work stops**.

2. Subordinate (dependent) clause cannot be used alone to express a complete thought; it must be attached to a principal (main or independent) clause.
   Example: **When it rains**, the work stops.

Uses: *SEVEN*
1. Noun clauses are used as nouns and are introduced by: who, whom, which, what, whether, if, whose, where, how, when, why, that, (sometimes "that" is missing but is an ellipsis)
   Example: **Why you never received my letter**, puzzles me. (subject)
   Example: I wonder whether (if) **she will come to the party.** (object)
   Example: We couldn't see from **where we sat.** (object of preposition)

2. Adjective clauses are used as adjectives and modify a noun or pro-

28

noun and are introduced by: who, which, that, as little as, such as, wherein, whereas, as many as, as much as
Example: The student **who failed** is repeating the course.

3. Adverb clauses are used as adverbs and modify a verb, adjective, or another adverb.
    Example: They will be happy **when we come.**

Special Clauses: *NINE—TWELVE*

1. Restrictive clause is a subordinate (dependent) clause which restricts the meaning of the principal (main or independent) clause.
    Example: Bananas **which are too ripe** are not good for eating.

Note: A restrictive clause is never set off by commas.

2. Non-restrictive clause is a subordinate clause which does not restrict the meaning of the principal (main or independent)) clause.
    Example: Mount Union College, **which is east of Malone College,** is a powerhouse in football.

Note: A non-restrictive clause is set off by commas.

SENTENCES

Definition: A sentence contains at least one subject (may be understood [ellipsis] and a verb which is sometimes called a predicate) *ONE*

Kinds:(construction)

1. A <u>simple</u> sentence has only one subject and one predicate, either or both may be compound. *ONE*
    Examples:
    Brown is a color.(simple subject)
    Red and **white** are the colors Santa wears. (compound subject) *TWO*
    I **eat** and **play** at noon.(compound predicate) *TWO*

2. A <u>compound</u> sentence has two or more principal (main or independent) clauses. *SIX*
    Example:

You came to English class today and **you learned.** (two joined sentences)

3. A <u>complex</u> sentence has one **principal (main or independent) clause** and one or more (dependent or subordinate clauses). *SEVEN*
   Examples:
   Dr.Cook, (who is our professor), **is from East Sparta, Ohio.**

   (If you learn grammar), **you need not feel ashamed to speak** (when you are in public).

4. A <u>compound-complex</u> sentence is a combination of **two or more principal (main or independent) clauses** and at least (one subordinate [dependent] clause).
   Example: **He wrote his essay** and **he took** **it to the "Write Place"** (where it was read). *EIGHT*

Kinds: (use)

1. Declarative
   Digits may be our toes or fingers or they may be the numbers 0—9.
   (Makes a statement to the reader) *FIVE*

2. Interrogative
   Which comes first lightening or thunder?
   (Asks your reader a question). *FIVE*

3. Imperative
   (You) Go to Malone College. (Ellipis) *FIVE*
   (Gives a command).

4. Exclamatory
   (Someone) Help! (Ellipis) *FIVE*
   (Shows strong feelings).

Chapter III

ROAD (reading) SIGNS ALONG THE WAY

- PUNCTUATION . ? !

- CAPITALIZATION

- SPELLING

- PREFIXES

- SUFFIXES

- ROOTS

- ROMAN NUMERALS

Chapter III

PUNCTUATION, CAPITALIZATION, SPELLING

PUNCTUATION
Use of the:
Period: (.)
1. after declarative and imperative sentences *ONE*
    Examples:
    A baby cow is a calf.
    Close the door.
2. after abbreviations *TWO*

Note: In ordinary writing avoid abbreviations and write out numbers whenever they can be expressed in not more than three words.

Note: In ordinary writing spell out all titles except Mr. Messrs.(plural of mister), Mrs., Dr., Ms., Jr., Sr. when used with proper names.
Example: Dr.Cook is a full professor of English. *TWO*
Example: The doctor is in the English Department. *TWO*

Abbreviations	Meanings *NINE—TWELVE*
anon.	anonymous
c. ca. circus	about (around) a given date
et al.(et alii)	and others
e.g. (exempli gratia)	for example
i.e. (id est)	that is
sic (sicundum)	thus (used after a quoted error p. 38)
a.m. (ante meridien)	before noon *THREE*
p.m. (post meridien)	after noon *THREE*
B.C.	before Christ
A.D. (anno Domini)	in the year of our Lord
B.C.E.	before the common era

viz. (<u>videlicet</u>)   namely
cf. (<u>conferee</u>)   compare
etc. (<u>et cetera</u>)   and so forth
vs.   versus
ibid. (<u>ibidem</u>)   in the same place
ff.   following
ed.   edited by or edition
No.   number p. 40

Note: Abbreviations are essential for research

3. to indicate the omission of words from a quoted passage *NINE—TWELVE*
    Example: "our fathers brought forth to this country..."

Note: APA and MLA and Chicago do not use the dots at the beginning. Use four dots if the quote ends the sentence.

4. in mathematical writing such as decimals (.01) and dollars ($5.00) *THREE*

Use of the <u>Comma</u>:(,)

1. Direct address *FIVE*
    Examples: **Daniel**, come here.

2. Series (word *THREE*, phrase *FOUR*, clause) *SEVEN*
    Examples:
    (a) In mathematics one must learn the terms **addend, quotient, and product**. (words)
    (b) Urban people live **inside a city**, suburban people live **outside the city**, and rural people live **in the farming country**. (phrases)
    (c) In mathematics an addend is one number added to another(3 plus 3 =6), and a quotient is one number divided by another(2 into 4 =2), and a product is one number multiplied by another(2 times 2=4). (clauses)

3. Direct quotation *THREE*
    Example:In his letter from Birmingham Jail, Martin Luther King Jr. wrote, "Society must protect the robbed and punish the robber."

4. Clauses (principal, main, or independent) **SEVEN**
   Separate the clauses of a long sentence with a comma.
   Example: I estimate (an educated guess) that the size of the room is
   15 feet by 20 feet, but I can't be certain until I measure it with a tape
   measure.

5. Clauses (subordinate or dependent) **SEVEN**
   Put a comma after the subordinate clause if it comes first in the sen-
   tence.
   Example: **If I give an "A" grade,** I expect "A" work.

6. Introductory words **NINE—TWELVE**
   Examples: **Yes,** I see.
   No, I didn't see.

7. Dates
   Example: **Monday, February 20, 1848.** **TWO**

8. Contrasting expression **NINE—TWELVE**
   Example: I will be graduated, **not in June,** but in August.

9. Unnatural order **NINE—TWELVE**
   Example: The student, **bored and tired,** slept.

10. Non-restrictive clause **NINE—TWELVE**
    Example: Clara Barton, **who founded the American Red Cross,**
    was a nurse.

11. Transitional words (parenthetical, not necessary) **NINE—TWELVE**
    Example: You, **of course**, must do your homework.

12. Word omission (ellipsis) **EIGHT**
    Example: I like chocolate; May, vanilla (likes is understood and is
    called an ellipsis).

13. City, state, country **THREE**
    Example: Canton, Ohio, USA

14. Salutation (friendly) letter **THREE**
    Example: Dear John,

15. Closing (complimentary ending of a letter) **THREE**

Example: Sincerely yours,

Note: The second word in a complimentary ending is not capitalized.

  16. Inverted name *NINE—TWELVE*
      Example: Cook, Martha

Use of the <u>Colon</u>:(:) *SIX*

  1. Salutation of a business letter
     Example: Dear Messrs.:

  2. Listing
     Example: I hit the ball three times: first, third and seventh innings.

  3. Biblical
     Example: Genesis 2:2

  4. Time *TWO*
     Example: 8:30 p.m.

  5. Mathematical *EIGHT*
     Example: 6:4::3:2 (ratio)
     6 is to 4 as 3 is to 2

Use of the <u>Semicolon</u>:(;)*SIX*

  1. Coordinating conjunction missing
     Example: Many people have the ability to write themes; others do not.

  2. Compound sentence joined by: also, so, thus, then, hence, besides, however, otherwise, accordingly, still, nevertheless
     Example: She is a fine lady; however, she sometimes gossips.

  3. Usually before explanatory expressions such as: thus, that is, namely, on the contrary, on the other hand, as (where used to introduce examples)
     Example: Four people were spoken of; namely, Jane, Fred, Jerry and Daniel.

Use of the <u>Question mark</u> (?) *ONE*

1. Interrogative sentence

2. Uncertainty *NINE—TWELVE*
    Example: He died January 15(?), 1945.

Use of the <u>Exclamation Mark</u>:(!) *TWO*

1. Exclamatory sentence (strong feeling)
    Example: "Forbid it, Almighty God!"

Use of the <u>Quotation Marks</u>:(" ") double or (' ') single *THREE*

1. Direct quotation *THREE*
    Example: Patrick Henry said, "give me liberty, or give me death!"

2. Direct quotation within a quotation (sometimes called an indirect quotation)
    Example: I said, "Patrick Henry said, 'give me liberty, or give me death!'" *FIVE*

3. A "special" word to be discussed *NINE—TWELVE*
    Example: Use the word "frequent" in a sentence.

4. A quotation more than one paragraph long will have quotation marks at the very beginning and at the very end.
    Example:
    > "Paragraph one.
    > "Paragraph two.
    > "Paragraph three."

Note: American Psychological Association (APA), Chicago and Modern Language Association (MLA) use indentation, double spacing and no quotation marks. *NINE—TWELVE*
    Example:
    > Paragraph one
    > Paragraph two
    > Paragraph three

5. Titles *NINE—TWELVE*

Short stories	"The Pearl"
Poems	"Ode to a Nightingale"
Articles	"I Inherited a Fortune"

Ships   "Queen Mary"

Use of <u>Parentheses</u>:( ) *SEVEN*

 1. The enclosed is for explanation.
   Example: If we have a vacation (and I know we will), I will visit you.
 2. The enclosed is to indicate alternative terms and omissions.
   Example: He (Bob) wrote this article.

Use of the <u>Dash</u> (—)*SEVEN*

 1. Sudden change in thought
   Example: He sighed and said—what did he say?
 2. Uninterrupted series of numbers
   Example: 1980—90 Chapter V—X

Use of the <u>Bracket</u>: [ ] **SEVEN**

 1. Correct a mistake from a quote
   Example: "Last night i [*sic*] found the door unlocked," he wrote.
 2. Functions as parentheses within parentheses
   Example: He wrote(Bowman Act [Sect. IV] of the law.

Use of the <u>Apostrophe</u>: (')*FIVE*

 1. Possessive case of nouns and indefinite pronouns
   Example: Men's room One's self *THREE*
 2. Omission of letters or numbers (contraction) *THREE*
   Example: It's

CAVEAT – A possessive pronoun never takes an apostrophe.

CAVEAT – Do not use an apostrophe to make numbers and letters plural
   unless it will be misunderstood (a's)
   Example: Ds 4s 1980s *FIVE*

Use of the <u>Hyphen</u>: (-)*SEVEN*

 1. Word division between syllables
   Example: Intro-duction

 2. Compound words

Example: sister-in-law

3. Combining words
   Example: happy-go-lucky

4. Numbers
   Example: Twenty-one through ninety-nine and in fractions such as one-quarter.

CAVEAT- Never divide a word of a single syllable.

Use of <u>Underlining</u> or *Italicization* (not both) ***NINE—TWELVE***

1. Titles of Books   <u>Gone with the Wind</u>

2. Foreign Words   *anno Domini*

3. Famous Ships   <u>Titanic</u>

4. Great works of art   <u>Blue Boy</u>

Use of the <u>Virgule</u>: (/) (commonly called a slash) ***NINE—TWELVE***

1. Separate alternatives
   Example: and/or

Note: APA MLA and Chicago do not accept the virgule.

Use of the <u>Caret</u> :(^) ***NINE—TWELVE***
1. Something is to be inserted.
   children's
   Example: The∧program was good.

CAPITALIZATION
Proper nouns.

1. Persons   Dr. Martha Cook ***ONE***
2. Places   Malone College ***ONE***
3. Organizations   Honor Society ***EIGHT***
4. Races (cultures)   Indian, African-***SEVEN***
   American, Caucasian

5.	Days, Months, Holidays	Monday, May, Christmas ***TWO***
6.	Historical periods	Before Common Era ***NINE***
7.	Events	World War I ***SIX***
8.	Documents	<u>Magna Carta</u> ***NINE***
9.	Deity	Lord, God, Almighty ***NINE***
10.	Titles of persons	Professor Cook ***THREE***
11.	Titles of books	(Do not capitalize a, an, the, or conjunctions and prepositions). ***FOUR***
12.	School subjects	Capitalize a subject ***SEVEN*** only if it comes from a country (English, England) or the subject has a Roman numeral after it (Algebra I)

CAVEAT - Abbreviations are capitalized only if the full word should be capitalized; the exception is number (No.) ***NINE—TWELVE***

Sentences
1. The first word of every sentence ***ONE***

2. The first word of every line of poetry ***TWO*** (There are exceptions called "poetic license").

Quotations
1. First word of every direct quotation ***FIVE***

Directions

1. North, East, South, West when they are sections of the country ***NINE—TWELVE***

Single letters
1. I, O when used as words ***ONE***

SPELLING *NINE—TWELVE*

PREFIXES (comes before)   **SUFFIXES** (comes after)

ambi - both *ambiance   able – fit *suitable
ante - before   age - state
anti - against   al - belonging to
auto - self   ance - act of
bene - well *benediction   ant – condition of
bi - two, twice   ary - place for *revolutionary
circum – around *circumference   er – one who has to do with
hemi – half *hemisphere   escue, esque style of
hyper - over, beyond   ful - having
inter – among   graph – written or drawn
intra - within   hood - condition
mal - bad   ist - profession
poly - many *polygon   ize - be, become
post - behind, after   less - lacking
pre - before *prediction   ly – manner *lively
semi - half   sub - under
ster – agent   tion - act of or process
super - above, over   tomy – cutting, incision
trans – across *transpiration   tude - state of being

ROOTS (located somewhere in the spelling of the word)

aqua – water   phon – sound *phonetics
aud - hear   port - carry
bio - life *biology   psycho – mind *psychology
chrono - time   rupt - break
dict - say *benediction   scop – see *telescope
duct - lead *conduct   scrib – write *scribe
fact - do, make *factory   serv - keep
flect - bent   solv - loosen
graph – write *autograph   tact - touch
hydro - water   tain - hold
ject - throw   tele – far *telescope
junct – join *conjunction   tract - pull
lect - read   ven - come
mitt - send   vert – turn *convert
morph – a change in physical   vid - see
     form *metamorphic   voc – call *vocal

mort – death   volv - turn around
ped - foot
pend – hang
*Note: Enlarge your vocabulary

SPELLING (some common rules)
Words with ie, ei *FIVE*
Do you wish to set your mind at ease about the correct spelling of over one thousand common words? Then memorize this bit of verse:

> Write i before e (niece)
> Except after c   (receive)
> Or when sounded like a
> As in neighbor and weigh.

Suffix: ***NINE—TWELVE***

> Rule: If a suffix begins with a vowel (a, e, i, o, u), drop the final e of the root word.
> Example: fame   famous

> Rule: If a suffix begins with a consonant, keep the final e.
> Example: entire entirely
> Exception: After c or g the final e is retained
> Example: courage courageous
>   notice noticeable

> Rule: Double a final single consonant before a suffix beginning with a vowel.
> A.   The consonant must be preceded by a single vowel.
> B.   The root should be one syllable or accent the last syllable.
> Example: slap   slapping

Check your spelling:
1. Is there a single final consonant?
2. Is there a single preceding vowel?
3. Does the suffix to be added begin with a vowel?
4. Is the last syllable accented?
   When the word checks out completely, double the final consonant.

> Rule: The final y is usually changed to i except before a suffix beginning with i.
> Example: happy   happi-ness
>   modify   modify—ing

FIVE   ROMAN NUMERALS *NINE—TWELVE*

I	=	1	L	=	50
II	=	2	C	=	100
III	=	3	D	=	500
IV	=	4	M	=	1,000
V	=	5	M̲M	=	2,000
VI	=	6	V̲	=	5,000
VII	=	7	X̲	=	10,000
VIII	=	8	C̲	=	100,000
IX	=	9	M̲	=	1,000,000
X	=	10			

CAVEAT: Be sure to put the line above the last four.
Try writing your complete date of birth in Roman numerals!
2/23/1926 II/XXIII/MCMXXVI

SPELLING (exercise to help in meaning and spelling) *NINE—TWELVE*

Learn to spell and know the difference in meaning.

accept, *except
advice, *advise
affect, *effect
all ready, already
all together, altogether
allowed, aloud
(<u>never</u> "out loud")
allusion, *illusion
ask, *asked
baring, bearing,*barring
berth, birth
born, borne
buy, by, bye
calvary, *cavalry
canvas, canvass
capital, capitol
choir, quire
chord, cord
cite, sight, site
close, *clothes, *cloths

know, no
later, *latter
lead, led
lessen, lesson
loose, *lose
mind,*mime, *mine
of, *off
(<u>never</u> "off of")
passed, *past
peace, piece
personal, *personnel
plane, plain
pray, prey
precede, *proceed
presence, presents
principal, principle
prophecy, *prophesy
quiet,quite
sense, *since
serf, surf

43

coarse, course
complement, compliment
conscience, *conscious
corps, core, *corpse
dairy, *diary
decent, *descent, *descend
desert, *dessert
device, *devise
dual, duel
dyeing, dying
fair, fare
formally, *formerly
forth, fourth, *forty
forward, foreword
hear, here
heard, herd
hole, whole
holy, wholly
irrelevant, *irreverent
its, it's
knew, new

shone, shown
staid, stayed
stationery, stationary
statue, *stature
steal, steel
straight, strait
than, *then
there, their, they're
threw, through,*thorough
(<u>do not</u> use "thru")
till, *until
to, too, two
track, *tract
troop, troupe
waist, waste
week, weak
weather, whether
which, witch
who, *whom
whose, who's
wright, right, rite
you're, your

Note: These are mostly homophones.
    * The asterisks denote these are not homophones.

Feel free to add to this list "new" words as you find them in your reading.

Chapter IV

OUTLINING UGH!

- Your readers can tell if you skipped this!
- I First main idea
-     A First subtopic of main idea
-         1. First division of subtopic
-             a. First detail of this division
-             b. Second detail of this division
-                 (1) Contributing detail (b)
-                 (2) Contributing detail (b)
-                     (a) Contributing detail(2)
-                     (b) Contributing detail(2)

CHAPTER IV

NINE—TWELVE

(Using what you have learned to make a speech or write a composition)

Choosing a Topic
1. If you are given a choice among a number of topics, choose the topic about which you (and your audience) are most interested and research material is readily available.

2. Narrow the topic to a specific part of that topic to keep within a time frame (speech) or composition (wordage).
    Example: Topic - Canines
    Specific – Collie Dogs

Organizing the Composition
1. Begin to organize your paper by "brainstorming" two or three main points you want to discuss about your topic.

2. Under each point, begin an outline of facts which will help develop that particular idea. Include any anecdotes, authorities, personal opinions, questions, and statistics which are pertinent. Use this form:
    I. First main idea (point)
        A. First subtopic of the first main idea
            1. First division of this subtopic
                a. First detail of this division
                b. Second detail of this division
                    (1) Contributing detail to this second detail (b)
                    (2) Another contributing detail to the second detail (b)
                        (a) contributing detail to (2)

(b) 2nd contributing detail
   2.   Second division of subtopic A
  B.   Second subtopic of the first main idea

CAVEAT: If you find yourself attempting to enter a single subheading, rearrange your outline to avoid it.

WRONG: I.   Winter sports
         A.   Football
            1. History
         B.   Skiing
            1. History

CORRECT: 1.   Winter sports
         A.   The History of Football
            1.   Origin
            2.   Growth
            3.   Present Status
            4.   Future Status
         B.   The History of Skiing
            1.   Origin
            2.   Growth
            3.   Present Status
            4.   Future Status

OUTLINE FOR A FACTUAL COMPOSITION (DATA) *NINE— TWELVE*

I.   Kinds of topics
   A. Natural sciences
      1.   Sciences of all kinds
      2.   Technology of all kinds
         a.   Inventions and how they are used
         b.   Results of their use
         c.   Possibilities for future use

   B. Social sciences
      1.   Arts
      2.   Government
      3.   Politics
      4.   Problems and interest of society in general

II. Research necessary for discussing the topics adequately
   A. Facts
      1. Information from wide reading
      2. Information from actually doing
      3. Information from thinking and analyzing
   B. Ability to draw conclusions from factual research

III. Personal skills needed to write the factual composition
   A. Ability to collect facts that prove a point
   B. Ability to hold the reader's interest
   C. Ability to present material clearly and logically
   D. Knowledge of technical vocabulary of the chosen field

IV. Methods used to develop a good paragraph
   A. Cause and effect
   B. Comparisons and contrasts
   C. Examples and illustrations
   D. Reasons
   E. Sufficient details

Note: These outlines may be used to evaluate written material or oral presentations.

Note: You may wish to use a complete sentence outline if you feel the need to teach complete sentences before you teach fragment outlining.

OUTLINE FOR A PERSONAL COMPOSITION (CREATIVE) *SEVEN*

I. Kinds of topics

   A. Subjects that require imagination
   B. Subjects that deal with personal experiences
   C. Subjects requiring creativity

II. Characteristics necessary for discussing the topic

   A. An interest in people and their reactions
   B. An accurate observation of everyday occurrences
   C. An analysis of your own and other's experiences

III. Skills needed to write the personal composition

A. A flair for vivid and colorful writing

    1. Unusual phraseology
    2. Picture-making words
    3. Personality revelation (appealing, clever, cute, humorous, witty)

B. Ability to make the reader visualize what you see
C. Ability to make the reader feel as you do
D. Ability to use imagination to create situations
E. Ability to philosophize about your experiences and reactions

IV. Methods of paragraph development

A. Cause and effect
B. Comparisons and contrasts
C. Examples and illustrations
D. Reasons
E. Details

WRITING A LONGER COMPOSITION *NINE—TWELVE* (A summation)

1. Work out a short introduction which contains the germs of your main points. Some experts go by this formula: tell your reader what you are about to say in the introduction, say it in the body, then tell them what you have just said in the conclusion.

2. Write each paragraph developing a point.

3. Develop the paragraph.

Note: In good compositions one should be able to read only the first and last sentences of each paragraph to get a skeletal meaning.

    (a) The first paragraph should contain a topic (thesis) sentence which should contain the content of the composition in the order of its reading and should be in the form of a noun and a verb plus their modifiers.

    (b) The last sentence of each paragraph should create interest for the paragraph to follow. Often this is achieved with a question.

(c) To develop the entire paragraph use some examples and illustrations, details, cause and effect, comparison and contrast and reasons.

(d) Write a one-paragraph conclusion which may contain personal opinions, suggestions, a summary, and or questions.

Note: All your compositions should be personalized; however, those who know the following skills will write more interestingly.

(a) Variety. Find different synonyms for the same words; vary transition words and phrases, etc. Use a Thesaurus.

(b) Vividness. Use specific details such as unusual (yet clear) phraseology, picture-making words (pinch of the needle) and let your personality come through (clever, humorous, witty, appealing words or phrases).

(c) Emotions. Make your reader feel exactly what you feel. Sometimes this is done with punctuation!

(d) Philosophy. Give an account of your reactions.

(e) Logic. Develop ideas logically following your topic (thesis) statement from your first paragraph.

USE THIS PAGE TO ANSWER ESSAY QUESTIONS IN YOUR OTHER SUBJECTS

1. Read the directions carefully so that you will recognize the key words.

2. Read carefully all the suggested topics if applicable.

3. Choose the one topic about which you have the most to say; you write best about the things you know best.

4. Reread carefully the wording of the title you have chosen to develop so that you will be sure to discuss the phrases inherent in the title.

5. Jot down on scrap paper two or three main areas of the topic.

6. Outline under each area facts which will develop the main point.

7. Include any quotations, statistics, authorities, anecdotes, or personal opinions that are pertinent.

8. Organize these points in their logical order.

9. Work out a short introduction that contains the germs of your main points. Write a thesis (topic) sentence which is a mini outline.

10. Write one paragraph developing one point; the next, developing your second point; if word limit permits, the third point.

11. Write a conclusion, which may be a summary, your personal point of view, or suggestions.

12. Reread your answer to check the correctness of technique. Use a *Thesaurus* when permitted.

13. Copy your perfected composition on to your answer paper. Be neat.

14. Reread what you have written (edit) and pray you have "aced" your essay answers.

CHAPTER V

- **FINDING MY OWN MISTAKES AND MAKING OTHERS MISERABLE FINDING THEIRS**

Are you an alumna or an alumnus?

Do you use lie and lay correctly?

Do you know when to use less and when to use fewer?

Who is a who and which is a which?

CHAPTER V

(Editing)

NINE—TWELVE

Some of the most common errors in usage:

A - used before words <u>except</u> those beginning with A, E, I, O, U (vowels)
An - used before words beginning with a vowel sound

Agree to - a plan
　　　　Example: I agree to your plan.
Agree with - a person
　　　　Example: I agree with you.

A half hour
Half an hour
A half an hour is always WRONG.

All of - use only with pronouns
　　　　Example: All of them were there.
All - use with nouns
　　　　Example: All the people were there.

Aloud - to be heard.
Allowed - to be permitted.
Out loud is always WRONG.

Alumnus - (singular masculine)
Alumni - (plural masculine)
Alumna - (singular feminine)
Alumnae - (plural feminine)

Among - more than two
> Example: Three boys fought among themselves.

Between - only two
> Example: The two boys fought between themselves.

And etc. used together is always WRONG.

As . . . as - a comparison with an affirmative statement
> Example: He is as bright as I am.

So . . . as - a comparison with a negative statement
> Example: He is not so bright as I am.

At - should not be used as the last word of a sentence

Burst is a verb
> Example: The balloon burst.

Bust is a noun
> Example: There is a bust of every inductee into the Football
> Hall of Fame in Canton,Ohio.

Can - to be able
> Example: I can make a kite.

May – permission
> Example: Mother, may I go shopping?

Can hardly - correct usage
Can't hardly - WRONG

Center on - not center around

Continual – broken in action
> Example: The continual dripping of water was drip,pause,
> drip, pause drip, pause etc.

Continuous - without breaking
> Example: The continuous sound of the siren went for one minute.

Could have - correct usage
Could of – **WRONG Note**: correct enunciation should remedy this.

Due to is usually an adjective
> Example: His tardiness was due to an accident.

Because of is usually an adverb.

Example: He was tardy because of his accident.

Differ with - means to disagree
　　Example: I beg to differ with you.
Differ from - means unlike
　　Example: I differ from you in height.

Famous - good connotation
　　Example: George Washington was a famous president.
Notorious - bad connotation
　　Example: Al Capone was a notorious criminal.

Feel bad - If you are sick or unhappy, you feel bad, not badly.

Few - can be counted
　　Example: If you have fewer than twelve items, use this cash register.
Less - degree, value, amount
　　Example: There was less snow last winter.

Good is never an adverb.
　　Example: She does her work well.

He doesn't, she doesn't, it doesn't is correct.
He (She, It) don't is **WRONG**.
Double negatives are always **WRONG**.
　　Example: He don't know nothing. **WRONG**
　　He doesn't know anything. CORRECT

In - means within
　　Example: I am in the room.
Into - from outside in
　　Example: I came into the room from the hall.

Its - possessive
　　Example: The dog lost its way.
It's – contraction
　　Example: It's (it is) a long way home.

Learn - acquire knowledge
　　Example: I learn from this book.
Teach - impart or give knowledge
　　Example: I can teach others from this book.

Let - permit, allow
>Example: Let me do that.

Leave - depart
>Example: Leave the room.

Lie - does not have a direct object.
>Example: Lie down on the bed.

Note: THE MEDICAL PROFESSION PEOPLE ARE THE WORST OFFENDERS OF THIS *FAUX PAS*.

Lay - does have a direct object.
>Example: Lay the book down.

Lose - something is missing.
>Example: Did you lose the pen?

Loose - something is not tight
>Example: The spring came loose.

Of – preposition Example: I am one of the officers.

Off – adverb Example: He ran off. (adverb)

Note: Off of is superfluous and is not used in formal writing.

Raise - animals
>Example: He raises rabbits.

Rear - children
>Example: She reared her children.

Regardless - correct usage

Irregardless - **WRONG**

Should have - correct usage

Should of – WRONG **Note**: enunciation should remedy this.

Sit - does not take a direct object
>Example: Sit still.

Set - does take a direct object
>Example: Set the vase here.

Note: EDUCATORS ARE THE WORST OFFENDERS OF THIS.

Than – is a comparison Example: I am better than he is.

Then – means time Example: I will finish this then I will come.

Stanza - the complete lines of a poem or music
    Example: Let's sing the first stanza.
Verse - one line only of a poem or song.
    Example: Let's rehearse the first verse.

Note: MUSICIANS ARE THE WORST OFFENDERS OF THIS.

This here, that there - **WRONG**

Unique - cannot be compared; one of a kind.
    Example: It is the most unique. **WRONG.**
    Example: It is the most nearly unique piece of furniture I have seen.

Note: THE SAME IS TRUE OF SUCH WORDS AS ROUND, SQUARE ETC.

Wait for - time lapses
    Example: I waited for him to begin.
Wait on - service
    Example. I waited on his table.

Who - refers to people
    Example: He is the one who came to the show.
Which - refers to things
    Example: That chair is the one which I like.
Note: MOST PEOPLE USE "THAT" BECAUSE THEY DON'T KNOW WHEN TO USE WHO OR WHOM.

You may wish to add to this list as you find errors in your own writing and speaking and that of those whom you are helping.

Chapter VI

- Call it what you want!
- Glossary

- Terminology

- Vocabulary of grammar

- There are other names you probably have used!

CHAPTER VI

(Glossary)

Grammatical Terminology

1. Abstract noun: a word that deals with concepts or ideas
    Example: He is known for his <u>honesty</u>. (p. 3)

2. Accusative: another name for objective case (p. 4)

3. Agreement: when the subject is singular, its verb must be singular
    Example: <u>Each has</u> his own book. (p. 8, 12)

4. Antecedent: a word or group of words to which a pronoun refers
    Example: This is the <u>man who</u> came to the house. (p. 8)

5. Appositive: denoting the same person or thing (p. 4)
    Example: Dr. Johnson, <u>Malone's president</u>, is a fine gentle man.

6. Articles: a, an, the- article adjectives (p. 8)
    a, an – indefinite article adjectives
    the - definite article adjective

7. Auxiliary: a verb that helps form a verb phrase (p. 10)
    Example: She <u>might be</u> president.

8. Caret: an inverted "V" that is used between two words in a sentence to point out an inserted word (^) (p. 39)

9. Case: the English language has three cases (p. 4, 5)
    subjective (nominative) see nouns and pronouns
    objective (accusative), possessive (genitive)

10. Clause a part of a sentence which contains a subject and a verb (p. 28)

11. Comparison: adjective or adverb change to indicate degrees of superiority in quality, quantity, or manner (p. 9, 19)
    (inflection)
    Positive(I thing)   good (adjective)
    Comparative(2 things)   better(adjective)
    Superlative(3 thing or more)   best(adjective)

    Positive(I thing)   happily (adverb)
    Comparative(2 things)   more happily (adverb)
    Superlative(3 thing or more)   most happily(adverb)

12. Complement: a word or words used to complete the sense of the verb
    Example: He brought a <u>book</u>. object (p. 4)
    Example: Sam is a <u>boy</u>. predicate noun (p. 4)
    Example: Sam is <u>handsome</u>. Predicate adjective (p. 10)

13. Conjugation: taking a verb through tense, voice, mood, number, and person (inflection) (p. 17)

14. Coordinate: joins words of equal rank (p. 21)
    Example: She <u>and</u> I are friends.

15. Copula: linking verbs (memorize these) (p. 10)

16. Correlative: a conjunction which is used in pairs (p. 21)
    Example: It is <u>either</u> a verb <u>or</u> a verbal.

17. Dash: a punctuation mark that is twice as long as a hyphen (p. 38)

18. Direct address: (vocative case in Latin) naming a specific person (p. 34)
    Example: Gordon, come here.

19. Direct quotation: the exact words someone says and the writer is quoting (p. 37)

20. Ellipsis: omitted words which are understood (p. 29)
    Example: Lana is prettier than I. <u>(am)</u>

21. Gender: masculine (male),feminine (female), neuter (p. 7)

22. Hyphen: half a dash (p. 38)

23. Idiom: an expression peculiar to a native language
Example: He made <u>no bones</u> about that. (see dictionary)

24. Inflection: change – noun is declension; verb is conjugation;
adjective and adverb are comparison
man   man's (p. 5)
do   did   doing   done (p. 11)
beautiful   more beautiful   most beautiful (p. 9)
heavily   more heavily   most heavily (p. 19)

25. Indirect quotation: a quotation within a quotation in which both double
and single quotation marks are used (p. 37)

26. Intensive: repeating a personal pronoun by adding self or selves to
strengthen the meaning (p. 6)

27. Mood (mode): the way a writer tells the reader whether the interpreta-
tion is a statement, a question or a command (p. 13)
Example: The sun set. (indicative)
Example: I wish I were sixteen again.(subjunctive)
Example: Do your work. (imperative)

28. Number: singular and plural (singular verbs with third person singular
pronouns have their verb ending in "s" (p. 12)
Example: He goe<u>s</u> to work.

29. Parenthetical: words that the author adds which have little meaning or value
Example: That, indeed, is right. (p. 35)

30. Parallel construction: using the same form throughout your sentence
such as dancing, playing, skating swimming or to dance, to play, to skate,
to swim–**do not mix the two**. (p. 22)

31. Parsing: tell everything grammatical about each word in a sentence.(Chp. 1)

32. Person: the English language has three persons (pronouns) (p. 7)
speaking   first person (I,We) see the boy.
spoken to second (You) see the boy.
spoken about third (She, He, It) sees the boy. singular
(They) see the boy. plural

33. Predicate adjective: an adjective used after a copulative (linking) verb and describes the subject.
    Example: The "Last Supper" painting is famous. (p. 10)

34. Predicate noun: a noun used after a copulative (linking) verb and is the same person (thing) as the subject see dictionary (p. 4)

35. Predicate pronoun
    Example: I am he. (p. 7)

36. Redundancy: repetition (p. 83)
    Example: Each (and everyone) will go.

37. Sentence: contains at east one subject and one verb and a complete thought (p. 29)

38. Subordinate clause: a part of a sentence that is of lesser status than the principal (main, independent) clause (a subordinate clause cannot be used as a sentence and will begin with a subordinate conjunction or a relative pronoun) (p. 28)

39. Syntax: the grammatical function of words, phrases, and clauses in a sentence (Chapter I, II)

40. Tense: indicates time of action of the verb (p. 11)
Present	I am
Past	I was
Future	I shall be
Present Perfect	I have been
Past Perfect	I had been
Future Perfect	I shall have been

41. Trite: boring from too much use (see dictionary)
    Example: (You know) (Cool).

CAVEAT: INTERVIEWEES ARE THE WORST OFFENDERS OF THIS.

42. Verbals: words that look like verbs but are used as nouns or adjectives (p. 13)

43. Virgule: a mark of punctuation often called a slash (p. 39)

44. Voice: (p. 13)

> Active subject does the acting
> Example: He hit the ball.
>
> Passive subject does not do the acting of the verb
> Example: The ball was hit by him.

APPENDIX A

- You learned when?
- You learned what?
- You learned where?
- Do you know why?
- Find it in this book!

COLOR CODING MATCHING OHIO STATE DEPARTMENT OF EDUCATION STANDARDS

GRADE ONE IS B	BROWN
GRADE TWO IS LT	LT. BLUE
GRADE THREE IS O	ORANGE
GRADE FOUR IS G	GREEN
GRADE FIVE IS R	RED
GRADE SIX IS DB	DARK BLUE
GRADE SEVEN IS L	LAVENDER
GRADE EIGHT IS BG	BT GREEN
GRADE NINE—TWELVE IS P	PINK

NOTE: Instead of color coding each line of this book, the grade level has been placed in bold print italics beside the item; this has been done to cut down on the cost of printing the book.

OHIO DEPARTMENT OF EDUCATION: ACADEMIC CONTENT STANDARDS K—12 ENGLISH LANGUAGE ARTS

Writing Conventions Standard: Students learn to master writing conventions through exposure to good models and opportunity for practice. Writing conventions include spelling, punctuation, grammar, and other conventions associated with forms of written text. They learn the purpose of punctuation; to clarify sentence meaning and help readers know how writing might sound aloud. They develop and extend their understanding of the spelling system, using a range of strategies for spelling words correctly and using newly learned vocabulary in their writing. They grow more skillful at using the grammatical structures of English to effectively communicate ideas in writing and to express themselves.

Benchmarks with guidelines for teaching grammar

KINDERGARTEN — BROWN
Punctuation and Capitalization
- Place punctuation marks at the end of the sentence.

GRADE ONE — BROWN
Punctuation and Capitalization
- Use end punctuation correctly, including question marks, exclamation points and periods.
- Use correct capitalization (e, g., the first word of a sentence, names and the pronoun I).

Grammar and usage
- Use nouns, verbs and adjectives (descriptive) correctly.

GRADE TWO — LIGHT BLUE
Punctuation and Capitalization
- Use periods, question marks, and exclamation points as end points correctly.
- Use quotation marks.
- Use correct punctuation for contractions and abbreviations.
- Use correct capitalization (e.g., proper nouns, the first word in a sentence, months, and days).

Grammar and Usage
- Use nouns, verbs, and adjectives correctly.

GRADE THREE — ORANGE

Punctuation and Capitalization:
- Use end punctuation marks correctly.
- Use quotation marks around dialogue, commas in a series, and apostrophes in contractions and possessives.
- Use correct punctuation for abbreviations.
- Use correct capitalization.

Grammar and Usage
- Use nouns, verbs, and adjectives correctly.
- Use subject and verbs that are in agreement.
- Use irregular plural nouns.
- Use nouns and pronouns that are in agreement.
- Use past, present, and future verb tenses.
- Use possessive nouns and pronouns.
- Use conjunctions.

GRADE FOUR — GREEN

Punctuation and Capitalization
- Use commas, end marks, apostrophes, and quotation marks, *(**parentheses**) correctly.
- Use correct capitalization.

Grammar and Usage
- Use various parts of speech such as nouns, pronouns, and verbs (e.g., regular and irregular, past, present and future).
- Use conjunctions and interjections.
- Use adverbs.
- Use prepositions and prepositional phrases.
- Use objective (accusative) and subjective (nominative) case pronouns.
- Use subjects and verbs that are in agreement.
- Use irregular plural nouns.

* omitted from original

GRADE FIVE — RED

Punctuation and Capitalization
- Use commas, end marks, apostrophes, and quotation marks correctly.
- Use correct capitalization.

Grammar and Usage:
- Use various parts of speech such as nouns, pronouns, an verbs (regular and irregular).
- Use conjunctions and interjections.
- Use adverbs.

- Use prepositions and prepositional phrases.
- Use objective (accusative) and subjective (nominative) case pronouns.
- Use indefinite and relative pronouns.

GRADE SIX — DARK BLUE
Punctuation and Capitalization
- Use commas, end marks, apostrophes, and quotation marks correctly.
- Use semicolons, colons, hyphens, dashes, and brackets.
- Use correct capitalization.

Grammar and Usage
- Use all eight parts of speech (e.g. noun, pronoun, adjective, verb, adverb, conjunction, preposition, interjection).
- Use verbs, including perfect tenses, transitive and intransitive verbs and linking (copulative)verbs.
- Use personal pronouns in subjective (nominative), objective (accusative) cases, and possessive, indefinite, and relative pronouns.
- Use subject-verb agreement with collective nouns, indefinite pronouns, compound subjects, and prepositional phrases.

GRADE SEVEN — LAVENDER
Punctuation and Capitalization
- Use commas, end marks, apostrophes, parentheses, and quotation marks correctly.
- Use semicolons, colons, hyphens, dashes, parentheses and brackets correctly.
- Use correct capitalization (both printing and cursive).

Grammar and Usage
- Use all eight parts of speech.
- Use subject-verb agreement with collective nouns, indefinite pronouns, compound subjects, and prepositional phrases.
- Use dependent and independent clauses.
- Conjugate regular and irregular verbs in all tenses correctly.

GRADE EIGHT — BRIGHT GREEN
Punctuation and Capitalization
- Use correct punctuation and capitalization.

Grammar and Usage
- Use all eight parts of speech.
- Use parallel structure to present items in a series and items juxtaposed for emphasis..

- Use clauses (e.g., independent [main, principal,] and dependent [subordinate] and phrases (e.g. gerundive, participial and infinitive).
- Use proper placement of modifiers.
- Maintain the use of appropriate verb tenses.
- Conjugate regular and irregular verbs in all tenses and moods correctly.

GRADE NINE — PINK
Punctuation and Capitalization
- Use correct punctuation and capitalization.
Grammar and Usage
- Use clauses (e.g., main [independent, principal] subordinate [dependent] and phrases (e.g., gerundive, infinitive, participial).
- Use proper placement of modifiers.
- Maintain the use of appropriate verb tenses (when to use the appropriate tenses).

GRADE TEN — PINK
Punctuation and Capitalization
- Use correct punctuation and capitalization.
Grammar and Usage:
- Use clauses (e.g. main [independent, principal], subordinate [dependent], and phrases (e.g. gerundive, infinitive, participial).
- Use parallel structure to present items in a series and items juxtaposed for emphasis.
- Use proper placement of modifiers.

GRADES ELEVEN AND TWELVE — PINK
Punctuation and Capitalization
- Use correct punctuation and capitalization.
Grammar and Usage
- Use correct grammar (e.g. verb tenses, parallel structure, demonstrative, reciprocal, reflexive[intensive], and interrogative pronouns).

"Standards are published by the Ohio Department of Education and used by permission. Use of the standards in this publication should be not construed as an endorsement of this publication by the Ohio Department of Education."

Note: Color coding each line has been eliminated to cut the costs of publishing this book; the author has put the numerical grade level in bold print italics at each pertinent item.

APPENDIX B

1. Just how
   much do you
   remember?

2. Just how
   much do you
   want to know?

3. Just how
   much do you
   need to know?

• Find it in this
  book!

Place the letter (A,B,C,D,E,F,G,H) on the line on the next page signifying the **part of speech** which matches the word that has a number over it.

In the autobiography of Frederick Douglas, a skilled

orator and writer, Douglas relates how he learned to read and

write. At first he was taught by the wife of his owner
                         1

because Frederick was a slave.
                   2

Next he was taught by the slave owner's children but

they didn't realize they were teaching him because

Frederick used their old textbooks.
                             3

Then Frederick went down to the docks and learned to
             4   5

read from the words printed on the huge boxes which came

into port. We don't realize how fortunate we are that we
                                      6

can learn to read and write if we so desire. It is too bad
                                    7

that we have so many advantages and yet some of us fail to

use them.

Grammar is one of those advantages which all people
            8   9

may learn if they choose to do so. It just takes perseverance

and desire and good instruction.
                              10

Frederick Douglas said, "Hallelujah, I learned to read

and write!"

_____1.   _____4.   _____7.   _____10.

_____2.   _____5.   _____8.

_____3.   _____6.   _____9.

KEY

A. noun
B. pronoun
C. adjective
D. verb
E. adverb
F. conjunction
G. preposition
H. interjection

Case of Pronouns—in the sentences below, choose the pronouns which would be correct in formal written English and write the correct pronoun in the blank to the left of the number. Guard against the idea that what is right is what sounds right; use the rules of grammar.

_____ 1. Who wants to read about Harry Potter? They all answered, "(Us, We)."

_____ 2. The work was divided between (him and I, he and I, him and me).

_____ 3. I am tired of (you, your) tattling on me.

_____ 4. I am older than (she, her).

_____ 5. May I speak to Holly? This is (her, she, me) speaking.

_____ 6. He would approve of (whomever, whoever) we chose as the secretary *pro tem* of the club.

_____ 7. I was having trouble with (he and she, he and her, him and she, him and her).

_____ 8. Among (we, us) four, there was total agreement.

_____ 9. It is (they, them, him, her) and not we who did the collage.

_____ 10. If I were (him, he), I would listen to the lecture.

Comparison (**positive, comparative and superlative**) of Adjectives and Adverbs—write the correct form found inside the parentheses on the line to the left of the number.

_____ 1. He did his work (good, well).

_____ 2. She sings the (louder, loudest) in the octet.

_____ 3. God made man (unique, most unique).

_____ 4. She bats third because she is the (most, more, less) likely to bring in the runners on first and second.

_____ 5. Of the two designers she is the (better, best, worst).

Recognition of **Phrases, Clauses and Sentences**—write the correct identification to the left of the number. Notice there is no mark of punctuation at the end; you may put in the correct punctuation on the ones which are complete sentences.

_____ 1. Tom Sawyer and Indian Joe are two of Mark Twain's (Samuel Clemens') characters

_____ 2. With many tries and many successes

_____ 3. Help

_____ 4. Since Harry Potter is my favorite character

_____ 5. "Jesus wept"

Use the **correct verbs** and pay close attention to principal part, tense, mood, and transitive or intransitive. Write the correct form to the left of the number.

_____ 1. The cornerstone was (layed, laid).

_____ 2. (Set, Sit) down.

_____ 3. If I (were, was) a congressman, I would do things differently.

_____ 4. Did you (loose, lose) your keys?

_____ 5. Once she had (did, done) the thesis sentence, she wrote the essay.

_____ 6. I (seen, saw) the movie "The Passion."

_____ 7. The picture was (hanged, hung) on the wall.

_____ 8. He (set, sat) on the chair.

_____ 9. She had (ate, eaten) all her spinach.

_____ 10. It (doesn't, don't) make any difference to me.

Agreement of **subject** with **verb** and **pronoun** with **antecedent**—put the correct form to the left of the number.

_____ 1. Either the two men or she (is, are) likely to be elected (i.e. for student council).

_____ 2. Not the administration, messrs. Bush and Chaney, and not labor but increasing automation in my opinion (is, are) the cause of unemployment.

_____ 3. The professor, with his students, (is, are) going on a field trip.

_____ 4. Members of the jury (sit, sits) in two rows.

_____ 5. The people in the audience (are, is) requested not to whistle at graduation.

_____ 6. Each member of the marching band is responsible for (his, their) musical instrument.

_____ 7. The year of our Lord, *anno Domini*, is abbreviated A. D. and, when followed by the year, (is, are) correct in biblical writing.

_____ 8. Ibid. means in the same place and is an abbreviation used by researchers and (it, they) prevent(s) redundancy.

_____ 9. Martin Luther King, Jr.'s famous speech *id est* (that is) "I Have A Dream" with its commentaries (are, were, is) a help for me to understand what he and all of us should wish.

_____ 10. Two drill sergeants put the squadron through (their, its) paces.

PUNCTUATION—write the letter which corresponds with the correct punctuation to the left of the number.

_____ 1. A. I said, "President Franklin Roosevelt said, 'We have nothing to fear but fear itself.'"
B. I said, 'President Roosevelt said, "We have nothing to fear but fear itself .'"
C. I said, President Roosevelt said, "We have nothing to fear but fear itself."

_____ 2. A. Lincoln, our sixteenth president, was a great man, however; he had much sorrow.
B. Lincoln, our sixteenth president, was a great man: however, he had much sorrow.
C. Lincoln, our sixteenth president, was a great man; however, he had much sorrow.

_____ 3. A. I had two lower case (ts) in that word.
B. I had two lower case (t's) in that word.
C. I had two lower case (t)s in that word.

_____ 4. A. The Red Badge Of Courage is a great book about war heroism.
B. The "Red Badge of courage" is a great book about war heroism.
C. The <u>Red Badge of Courage</u> is a great book about war heroism.

_____ 5. A. The beaker was three-fourths full of acid.
B. The beaker was three fourths full of acid.
C. The beaker was three/fourths full of acid.

CAPITALIZATION Write the letter to the left of the number which corresponds to the correct capitalization.

_____ 1.   A.   Yours Truly,
             B.   yours truly,
             C.   Yours truly,

_____ 2.   A.   The title of the book is <u>Gone with the Wind</u>.
             B.   The title of the book is "Gone With the Wind."
             C.   The title of the book is " Gone with The Wind."

_____ 3.   A.   I never took Algebra.
             B.   I took Algebra I.
             C.   I never took algebra I.

_____ 4.   A.   James told me to go North two blocks and then turn East.
             B.   James told me to go east two blocks and then turn North.
             C.   Allen told Ruth that the West was beautiful.

_____ 5.   A.   Abraham Lincoln said, "Our fathers brought forth to this country."
             B.   I said,". . . .go home."
             C.   I said to my Dad, "I am going to Malone College."

EDITING: Write the letter found at the bottom of the page beside the number which correctly identifies what each sentence illustrates.

_____ 1.   Childhood is an exciting interesting, bustling, seeking time of life.
_____ 2.   The milking stool was made by a man with three legs.
_____ 3.   Miriam she made the vase from clay.
_____ 4.   Write and print legibly.
_____ 5.   Carl said, "Edgar Allen Poe said, 'Quoth the raven never more.'"
_____ 6.   If I were not a Christian, I might be tempted.
_____ 7.   He made no bones about his feelings.
_____ 8.   A surprise party was given for me.
_____ 9.   He is the clown.
_____ 10. When I say, women are mammals and mares are mammals, I know I am correct because both have *mammalia*.

A. Compound–complex sentence; B.Dangling (misplaced) modifier; C.Ellipsis; D.finite verb; E.Indirect quotation; F.Parallel construction; G.Passive voice; H. Redundancy; I.Subjunctive mood; J.Third person masculine; K.idiom

SPELLING—Write the letter which is beside the correct spelling to the left of the number.

_____ 1. I am not _____pleased that you as an alumna(female graduate)and you as an alumnus(male graduate) do not have your credentials _____ in one notebook.
A. altogether, all together
B. altogether, alltogether
C. all together, all together
D. altogether, altogether

_____ 2. The grammatically correct check-out register sign read, "_____than twelve items."
A. less
B. lesser
C. few
D. fewer

_____ 3. He did _____ on his test because he has _____ study habits.
A. good, good
B. well, good
C. well, well
D. good, well

_____ 4. He had ____many things on his mind and ___little time ____ do them.
A. to, to, to
B. too, too, to
C. to, to, too
D. too, too, too

_____ 5. Sigmund Freud, ____most of us have read about, was a psychologist _____wrote many books.
A. who, who
B. whom, whom
C. whom, who
D. who, whom

_____ 6. The abandoned kitten lost ___ way but ____ the owner who
finally found it.
A. it's, its
B. its, it's
C. it's,it's
D. its, its

_____ 7. _____clothing over ____is much more expensive.
A. Thier, there
B. There, their
C. Their, there
D. There, thier

_____ 8 ._____is not a difficult thing to learn if _____ diligent in cor-
recting past mistakes from a reliable source.
A. Grammar, you're
B. Grammer, you're
C. Grammer, your
D. Grammur, your

_____ 9. I couldn't catch _____the tense of verbs until I
ran_____this book which is called *Grammar toward profes-
sonalism.*
A. onto, on to
B. on to, on to
C. onto, onto
D. on to, onto

_____ 10. The _____of mass learning is not as profitable as the
_____of distributed learning but sometimes both kinds of
learning_____my personality.
A. effect, affect, effect
B. affect, effect, affect
C. effect, effect, affect
D. affect, affect, affect

KEY TO GRAMMAR TEST

Parts of speech one point each
1. D verb
2. G preposition
3. E adverb
4. C adjective
5. G preposition
6. E adverb
7. B pronoun
8. F. conjunction
9. A noun
10. H interjection

Case of pronouns 2 points each
1. We
2. him and me
3. your
4. she
5. she
6. whomever
7. him and her
8. us
9. they
10. he

Comparison of adjectives and adverbs and recognition of phrases, clauses, and sentences one point each
1. well
2. loudest
3. unique
4. most
5. better

1. sentence
2. phrase
3. sentence
4. clause
5. sentence

Verbs one point each
1. laid

2. Sit
3. were
4. lose
5. done
6. saw
7. hung
8. sat
9. eaten
10. doesn't

Agreement of subject and verb and pronoun and antecedent two points each

1. is
2. is
3. is
4. sit
5. are
6. his
7. is
8. it
9. is
10. its

Punctuation one point each

1. A
2. C
3. A
4. C
5. A

Capitalization and editing one point each

1. C
2. A
3. B
4. C
5. C

Editing

1. F
2. B
3. H
4. C
5. E
6. I
7. K
8. G
9. J
10. A

Spelling one point each

1. A
2. D
3. B
4. B
5. C
6. B
7. C
8. A
9. D
10. C

APPENDIX C

- Know the vocabulary of the subject you are studying.

- The same word may have different meanings depending on the use in the sentence.

- The same word may have different meanings depending on the subject being discussed.

Third and fourth grade elementary teachers listed these "key" vocabulary words as used in standardized testing. Many of these words have been incorporated into the model sentences in *Grammar Toward Professionalism*.

Third grade list:
ADDEND
ADJECTIVES
ADVERBS
ANCESTOR
CAPITALIZE
CLASSIFY
COMPARE
COMPASS
CONCLUSION
CONGRUENT
CONGRUENCE
DIFFERENCE
DIVISION
ENVIRONMENT
ESTIMATE
FACTOR
FORCE
FOSSIL
HYPOTHESIS
IGNEOUS
INVESTIGATE
METAMORPHIC
MINERAL
MOTION
MULTIPLICATION
NOUNS
OBSERVE
ORDER
PRODUCT
PREDICTION
PRODUCTION
PROPERTIES
RETELL
SEDIMENTARY
STATEMENT
SUM
SUMMARY
URBAN
VERBS

Fourth grade list:
ADDEND
ARCHAELOGIST
CHARACTERISTICS
CONSUME
CONSUMPTION
CONTRAST
DIGIT
ECOLOGY
ENTREPRENEURSHIP
ENVIRONMENT
FACTOR
FRACTIONS
GOVERNMENT
HEMISPHERE
HOMOPHONES
IMMIGRATION
INDEPENDENT
METAMORPHOSIS
OCEANOGRAPH
ORGANISMS
PERIMETER
PHOTOSYNTHESIS
PLANE
POLYGON
PRODUCE
PRODUCT
PRODUCTION
PURPOSE
REFERENCE
RESOURCES
SEGREGATION
SUFFIXES
SUMMARIZE
SYMBIOSIS
TRANSPIRATION
UNDERGROUND RAILROAD
SYMMETRY

APPENDIX D

- Authors sometimes slip words into the text from a different language.
- Don't skip them!
- Learn what they mean.

- Now you are multilingual!

FOREIGN WORDS SOMETIMES USED IN AMERICAN LITERATURE

LATIN

ad hoc temporary issues
ad nauseum becoming ill
alma mater bounteous mother
anno Dominus in the year of the Lord
Ave Maria hail Mary
bona fide real
Caveat emptor! Let the buyer beware.
Caveat lector! Let the reader beware!
Cave quid dicis! Beware what you say!
E pluribus unum one out of many
genesis beginning
Homo sapien mankind
in absentia not present
magna cum laude with great praise
mens sana in corpore sano a sound mind in a sound body
opus work
per se by itself
semper fidelis always faithful (loyal)
semper paratus always prepared
status in quo the existing state
summa cum laude with greatest praise
Tempus fugit Time flies
terra firma solid ground
Veni, Vidi, Vici! I came, I saw, I conquered!

FRENCH

bon appetit good appetite
bona fide real
bon jour good day
déjà vu already considered
faux pas mistake, blunder
garçon young man(waiter)
laissez faire freedon of choice
moi me
N'est-ce pas? Is it not?
oui yes
s'il vous plait if you please
tres bien very good
vis-à-vis face to face

OTHER

dolce sweet (Italian)
shalom peace (Hebrew)

SPANISH

adios good bye
amigo(a) friend
gracias thank you
mañana tomorrow
numero number
¿Quien sabe? Who knows?
si yes
uno one
kemosabe friend

GERMAN

Dummkopf dumb head
Edelweiss white flower
Frau wife
Gesundheit healthiness
Kinder children
wunderbar wonderful

APPENDIX E
GENRE

- BIBLIOTHERAPY
  Decision making
- DRAMA
  Verbal and non
  verbal
- ESSAY
  Opinion
- PARABLE
  Creative
- NONFICTION
  Historical
- POETRY
  Literature in
  verse

BIBLIOTHERAPY

This story was read to a group of kindergartners after two of them decided to remove their clothes to check out the anatomy of the other.

Best Friends

Did you know that little puppies have daddies? Yes, they do. I am going to tell you a story about two puppies and two daddies.

One puppy was a mischievous little fellow named Socks. He had black fur but his little feet were white and he looked as if he were wearing socks. His daddy was a furry dog who really took good care of Socks even when Socks did things he shouldn't have done. Socks' daddy was called Bobby because at one time he had been a police dog. Did you know that in a far off England, policemen are called Bobbies? But Socks didn't call his daddy, Bobby; he called him daddy because that is what he should be called when he is your daddy.

Not very far away in another family was a puppy named Captain, but he was nicknamed Cappie. Cappie was a nice puppy but at times Cappie was a bit bossy. Sometimes Captains must be bossy. Cappies's daddy was a big black and white dog who had been a dog that rode on fire trucks. Have you seen pictures of fire trucks with black and white dogs riding along? Cappie's daddy's name was Carson but Cappie called his daddy "Arson" because it was hard to say Carson. That was not a good name to call Carson because arson means some one has set something on fire that should not be burned. Carson's daddy told Cappie not to call him Arson but to call him Daddy.

One day the two puppies were playing together and Cappie got a bright idea! He asked Socks if he would take off his bright silver collar which had the name "Socks" on it. A collar on a dog is his clothes. Socks knew he was not supposed to take off his collar but Cappie insisted. Cappie was bossy and sometimes would get his best friend into trouble. Cappie took his collar off and then dared Socks to do the same. Both puppies knew it was wrong because that collar had an important purpose. It was their entire wardrobe and told others about them if necessary. Socks was a follower and wanted to keep Cappie as his friend. Sometimes we have to decide what is right—not what might be popular.

While they were playing, two little boys came along and each one took a puppy thinking they were strays because the puppies had taken off an important item—their identity.

The boys were on their way to taking the puppies home when Socks realized he should never have taken off his collar— he was now in strange territory! Sock's jumped from the boy's arm and ran and retrieved his collar. Cappie reluctantly did the same thing—he never liked to be wrong. The puppies outran the boys and went home carrying their respective collars.

When Socks returned home, he asked his dad to help him put his collar back on. Bobby asked Socks why he was not wearing his collar. Socks replied that Cappie had talked him into removing his collar. Bobby told Socks that when he knew that things were wrong, he should not do as others do. Bobby told Socks that this was a good lesson to learn and that all puppies (even people) had to learn. From now on Socks should not let others (even friends) talk him into doing things he knew were not right.

Cappie didn't tell his dad, Carson, about the removal of the collar but Carson learned about it from Socks' dad, Bobby.

Carson asked Cappie why he would want to remove his collar and why he would want his best puppy friend to do the same? Cappie said he just thought it would be fun. Now he knows that thoughtless fun can get one into dangerous trouble. Puppies wear collars so that people know they have owners and homes. Without the collars the puppies might never have returned home.

Carson said that Cappie should remember that collars to puppies and dogs are like clothes to real people. They should be worn at all times unless daddy or mommy tells them to remove them for special occasions like baths and bedtime. Carson and Bobby talked with Cappie and Socks and the two puppies became friends again. Cappie learned not to be so bossy and Socks learned that he should not do what others say when he knows it is wrong.

Now the puppies can play together with their shiny collars in place. It is hard to grow up but we all must do it in time. Dr. Martha J.B. Cook

Now let us discuss the choices we have when someone suggests something that we should or should not do.

BIBLIOTHERAPY

Are You a Long Distance Runner?

This essay may be used as a preface to "senioritis" or for any student who seems to "slack off" toward the end of the year.

A sprinter starts fast and speed takes him or her a short distance. A relay runner passes the stick to the next runner. A long distance runner places a premium on endurance, an economical running style, which sets an achievable pace to finish the race. Long distance runners train with discipline called fartlek which consists of daily workouts on surfaces such as sand which may impede their progress. Sometimes they run uphill to test their strength. In training they seldom run on a smooth, rubberized surfaces on which competition is held. Why? Because the runner must endure hardship to make certain that when the way is smoother, he or she will have the strength in reserve to finish.

Paul(Saul) was a long distance runner. His trainer was Hillel's grandson, Gamaliel, who taught Paul the importance of saving energy for the finish of life's race. Paul took those teachings and converted them to Christianity. Paul pulled in the poles of his ancient world and bound them to the cross. "I have made you a light to the Gentiles, to lead them from the farthest corners of the earth to my salvation" Acts 13:47). From Italy to Syria he blazed the trail for Christ. In Macedonia, Thrace, Greece, Asia Minor, Galatia, and Pisidia. In Bithymia, Pontus, Cappadocia, Cilicia, Syria, Cyprus, and Idumea he threw open to us the doors of the Christian Church and ask us to come in. Along the race this long distance runner was whipped, stoned, starved, frozen, ship-wrecked, half drowned, and finally beheaded. He had won the race; he had reached the goal of eternal life.

Are you a long distance runner or are you a sprinter who can't make the distance or are you a relayer who passes the duties to someone else? "After all, salvation is not given to those who know what to do, unless they do it" Romans 2:15. You can learn to change from a non-racer, to a sprinter, to a relayer, to a long distance runner and, like Paul, blaze a trail for Christ and then let's all get together in heaven. "I strain to reach the end of the race and receive the prize for which God is calling us up to heaven because of what Christ Jesus did for us" (Philippians 3:14).

Dr. Martha J. B. Cook

DRAMA

Poetry to be narrated and then acted in a dramatic fashion.

THERE'S MORE TO COOKING THAN THE RECIPE

We got together eight cooks and I.
We're not actors and you shall see why.

We can't sing and we can't act,
But we can cook and that's a fact.

There's a message we want to tell
About some things that should be done well.

We know we are good but we want to be better.
We try to obey rules—down to the letter.

There's an old saying we serve with our meals—
What's not in your head must be in your heels.

Miss inefficiency is making a cake;
Get ingredients together before you bake.

She remembered the bowl but forgot the flour,
Off to get it—it takes her an "hour"!

She starts again—she forgets the eggs,
This poor soul is sure using her legs.

This time the pans—off she goes
Across the kitchen—using legs, heels and toes.

The cake is completed — but wasn't that silly?
If she'd just planned ahead, no willy nilly.

Now Miss efficiency does the same chore,
Her tools are handy—she needs no more.

She completes her task; she's way ahead.
She saves her heels—used her head instead.

We need our cooks—we need them each day.
We want them intact—we like them that way.

Sometimes we have spills—safety we stress,
But Miss Careless Cook didn't wipe up her mess.

She took a fall—she's out for a day.
She sprained her arm; she also lost pay.

Miss Safety First—cleaned up her dirt,
Doesn't that make sense? She didn't get hurt.

Grooming's important; no hairs in the soup.
We want to look nice—we don't want to droop.

Miss Stylish forgets that while she is standing
Her skirt looks good, by her knee it is landing.

But let her bend over, how that hem rises!
Her audience is in for some "pleasant" surprises.

Miss Modesty wears her dresses the same.
But she knows how to stoop—now there's no blame.

She also knows tightness is for skin
Not for the dress that she finds herself in.

Things can go wrong and tempers can flare.
Miss Lacking patience—she's to beware.

If things break down and she's not on time
The words she says can't be put in this rhyme!

But Miss Patience Plus takes it all in her stride;
She asks help from others and they come to her side.

She thanks them for helping in time of her need.
We're all good Samaritans; let that be our creed.

How you meet a crisis might well tell the tale
Of success in endeavor or how one can fail.

With one piece of meat and three more to feed
You cut it in thirds, now you've got what you need.

Though ration be scrimp and you've served to the limit,
There's nourishment plenty if a smile is put in it.

Women are women and God bless them all.
But Eve has been blamed for Adam's fall.

She said the wrong thing; she talked out of turn.
She hadn't heard what we all must learn.

Talking is fine if kept in its place;
If no, then we must put gags on our face.

Talk and be friendly; say something good,
Otherwise; just keep your mind on the food.

We hope you have liked our lessons in rhyme.
We also hope you've had a good time.

Dr. Martha J.B. Cook

This has been used a number of times and is very flexible in making the drama as funny or as serious as one wishes. The narrator is an important part of this kind of poetry in drama. This can be made into a great parody on other kinds of work—even homework.

ESSAY

MONKEY SEE—MONKEY DO

This essay was written to be controversial among generations. Perhaps it will show how we succumb to fads as we progress through life and each generation reflects on the folly of following the crowd. An essay may express an opinion and should have an element of debate in it.

I have lived long enough to see many different fads in clothing and how it is worn. In some of them I was the "Monkey Do."

In the 40s it was bobby sox pulled up as high on the legs as they would go and were usually white. I had to wash mine in the sink each night because I had only one pair and knee sox was a social ostracism. The real innovation of the 40s was to wear a cardigan backwards with a white tailored blouse with the collar straight up. I did not have a white tailored blouse but my older brother had a white shirt. Who cared if it buttoned the wrong way? I never took off my cardigan so my secret was safe. Being "with the gang" mattered most and that taught me to be resourceful.

Then came WWII and the United States could not buy any imports from Japan. That took care of the silk hose that had been plentiful before the war. Nylon was not yet available. Entrepreneurism came up with a tube of color to dye the legs and it looked pretty authentic even though every one knew it was a dye because nearly everyone resorted to the dyed legs. The dyed legs had two drawbacks that needed to be addressed. Silk hose always had a seam down the back. I overcame that obstacle by using my eyebrow pencil (sometimes the seam was quite wavy). The second obstacle was the fact that the color came off on the sheets at night. Mother wanted me to wash it off before I went to bed but it took too long to put it on in the morning—especially the "seam." I convinced her that I liked mottled tan sheets.

Enough about me. What about you of the 21st century? Where did you get the idea that bib overalls were dressy—especially when it was the "thing" to allow the right or left shoulder strap unfastened. In my naiveté I never figured out what the message was as to the code for right or left. I'm certain there was one just as there seems to be a code for which ear the sole earring is placed.

Next the overalls went to jeans which, at first, were cut from a thong pattern which gave the girls "wedgies" and the legs were cut three inches too long for the boys. Many a girl had much discomfort with the tight jeans and many a floor was made cleaner by the abrasive jean material covering the shoe soles. Those fads I never figured out along with untied shoelaces which wiggled from the too long pants and tried hard to trip the wearer.

I don't want this essay to be so long as to lose the limited concentration of its readers. Two more 2000s fads have caught my eye.

The plumber in the advertisement who displays the crevice in his derriere must have promoted the "low cut" jeans for both men and women. When I see that ad, my mind becomes mischievous and I would like to use my camera to show the guilty how one looks in the low cut attire. Perhaps the "Monkey See—Monkey Do" is an affront to the Monkey.

I think the very worst "Monkey See—Monkey Do" was epitomized when I recently attended a banquet—(not formal but dress nicely)–perhaps that is an oxymoron! Our waitress, a sweet young lady in her late teens, was wearing a blouse that was at least two sizes too small and the neckline showed a replica of the crevice displayed by the plumber only on a different part of the anatomy. You haven't read it all! While she was serving guests, her navel ring, obviously displayed, got caught in the napkin on the tray she was carrying and jiggled a cup of hot coffee onto her bare midriff. The young lady took the burn rather than drop the tray. What stoicism she displayed!

Probably the readers of this essay have moved to new fads. Challenge me in your essay and defend what your generation is accepting in apparel.

Dr. Martha J.B. Cook

ESSAY

THE WHOOPEE CUSHION SHOES

This essay was written to bring to light the fact that many times things aren't what they seem. People are often blamed for conditions that may exist in our minds but are not actualities when the whole truth is known.

I am not the only one this has happened to but I am the only one brave enough to write about it.

Last summer I bought a pair of black shoes with air insoles. I have trouble getting shoes wide enough through the toes and narrow enough through the heal. Consequently, the toes win out and the heal rises up and down in and out of the shoes as I walk. At the store I tried on the right shoe and it felt so good I immediately said, "I'll take this pair," and never tried on the left shoe.

I wore my new shoes for the first time in the classroom when I taught summer school. I walked down the hall and several people whom I passed began to laugh. It was then I heard that this whoopie sound was coming from my left shoe as my heel lowered itself into the shoe. Later I mentioned this to my husband as to how terribly embarrassed it made me feel.

He listened to me walk in those shoes and he is quite blunt. "That sounds just like you are passing air." However he used the four letter word. "I suppose people try not to laugh just to be polite but it certainly sounds like the real thing.

I didn't wear those shoes for a while and then I happened to take another pair to the shoe repair and I mentioned my dilemma. The shoe man said, "I can fix that," so I gave him my left shoe. He took only a few minutes and I wore the shoe home.

A little while latter I wore those shoes to an English class that I was teaching. Suddenly, the left shoe began to make the whoopie noise.

Immediately I left the room and went to the rest room and dampened the shoe. I came back to class and the noise happened again and again. I noticed some of the class was politely trying to stifle a snicker. I didn't know how to explain.

Actually, I am passing air but not in the anatomical part for which I am being ridiculed.

Would you throw the shoes away; get them fixed again; be embarrassed again when the shoe makes the passing air sound or would you be mean and give them to another person without telling that person of the flaw in the shoe? I still have the shoes! Help me decide.

Dr. Martha J.B. Cook

PARABLE (FICTION)

The Parable of the Transplant

It probably would not be a good idea to have anyone below college status write a parable unless it would be an Advanced Placement (Gifted) high school English class. Writing a parable is difficult and it makes one have tremendous respect for Jesus because this was His strategy for much of His teaching.

A famous surgeon and a highly successful lawyer sat across from each other in the lawyer's office. They were discussing a most unusual lawsuit. It seems that a wealthy young lady had come to the surgeon and asked if the surgeon could, by means of a transplant, make her an instant success. She did not want to go through the tedious and time consuming task of learning everything needed to be a success. Surely there must be some way that the surgeon could transplant a new memory bank to her brain so that she would have instant learning and consequently instant success. The surgeon pondered the idea, but before he would consent, he asked the help of the lawyer to draw up an executory contract. In this contract was stated that the surgeon would transplant a cerebral cortex onto the cerebrum in her brain. The cerebral cortex controls the skilled movements of the eyes, the keen memory of past experiences, the detailed movements of the hands, and the persuasive powers of speech. The contract further stated that the transplant would take place as soon as the lawyer had found a suitable donor.

The lawyer searched and researched for a suitable donor. Sometimes he would find a donor with a keen memory, but the power of persuasive speech was missing. Or maybe he would find a skilled workman whose hands were well coordinated, but his memory was poor. It took a concentrated search to find the right cerebral cortex. The man was aged and had a relatively short time to live. The lawyer had interviewed the aged man's long-time friends; "Yes, he was very keen sighted."

His relatives said, "Yes," to his photographic memory and "he never forgot a thing!"

His acquaintances attested to the fact that his manual dexterity and power of persuasive speech had always been "unusually gifted and most convincing."

In time the transplant was performed and the wealthy client received the new cerebral cortex or—in common terms—a new memory bank. The surgeon's skill was acclaimed! The client had fully recovered! Why then was the client suing the surgeon and the lawyer? Had the client changed her mind? (pun intended)

The client was suing the lawyer because of the donor he chose, and the surgeon because he was an accessory to the contract. The client, eager to test her instant success, viewed her surroundings with her new keen eyesight, but she saw only ugliness; she could not see beauty. She used her great power of persuasive speech, but all she could utter were negative curses; she could not speak wholesome truths! What had happened? I think we biblical scholars know. The lawyer had neglected to ask the donor's long-time friends HOW the donor had used his keen sight, had not ask the donor's family WHAT the donor remembered, and had not inquired of the donor's acquaintances HOW the donor's manual dexterity and persuasive speech had been trained to be used. Are you that donor? As Nathan said to David, "You are that man!" (2 Sam. 12:7).

Dr. Martha J.B. Cook

HISTORY (non fiction)

Funny Things Happened to Me on the Way to Retirement

Autobiographies are history and they don't necessarily need to be one's entire life to date. It is interesting to choose various parts of one's life and write one's own personal history or non fiction.

Because of circumstances I was permitted to go into the first grade in a one-room schoolhouse when I was barely five years old. The work was easy; the amenities were difficult. I was afraid of the half moon facility down the hill. Immature bladders become full quickly! I emptied mine on my seat and onto the floor. When I was asked by the all-knowing teacher what had happened, I promptly replied, "This roof leaks." Ever since, I have been known to reply to inquiries which surprise the hearer.

The one-room school was abandoned in midyear—right before the chimney collapsed next to where I sat in a seat in which my legs dangled and swung all day long to the beat of voices at the recitation bench.

The "new" school to which we were assigned was far away and we no longer could walk to school. The first day of riding the school bus, I fell off the long bench-like seat which lined the wall underneath the windows and faced the seats which lined the other side of the bus. I had no anchor because my feet could not touch the floor and there were no armrests. I lost my lunch which mother had carefully wrapped in yesterday's newspaper. I picked it off the floor where many a foot had trod and put it back in the newspaper and stuffed it where my breasts would eventually be. Mother wondered about the stains on the **inside** of my blouse. I actually told her the truth about how they got there.

Teachers do not like "new" students coming into their classrooms in the middle of the year. Most teachers feel that the "new" students are retarded because they did not have the benefit of their expert teaching. My new teacher during the second week of our new surroundings, which were in the back of the room, asked if any one could say the alphabet backwards. I immediately raised my hand and my fellow neighbors from the one-room school gasped at my calling her bluff. They knew, as I knew, that she was attempting to prove her belief that we came retarded in the work that she had taught her deeply entrenched students. My colleagues also felt that I was going to make them look bad because they thought I would stumble after the z,y,x. I didn't stumble — I read it backwards off the chart displayed over the chalkboard! I don't know to this day if she caught on because I was clever enough not to stare at my prompt. I thoroughly enjoyed being a celebrity to my classmates.

We went to high school in the seventh grade because the district had no junior high. I was made to take home economics which I detested. One day during my eighth grade year the principal came and pulled me out of class. He didn't take me to his office; he nose-faced me in the hallway so that many of my friends who were now changing classes could see I was in a predicament. I sensed they smiled as they went past because I was miss "goody two shoes" to them. This was because mother lived the adage, "Get into trouble in school; you are in trouble at home." The principal handed me numerous sheets of sandpaper and ordered me to sand the inside bottom of the drawers on six home economics tables. I later learned that my name had been penciled on one of the drawers. I did the sandpapering during lunch period and two study halls. That night my mother asked me why I did not bring my clarinet home from school as I always did. I had to maintain my first chair status so I practiced every night. Sometimes I practiced in the chicken house when Dad, who was a traveling salesman and was home only on weekends, somehow didn't like my music. I told mother the pads of my fingers were raw from sandpapering and I couldn't stand the pain when applied to the holes of my instrument. I reluctantly told mother the story and mother immediately called the president of the school board. Mother knew I would never deliberately mar something that did not belong to me. I tried never to mar anything that did belong to me! After several days the principal and the home economics teacher came to me and apologized. Years later I taught for that principal and he apologized again and admitted that he learned to get "all sides of the story" before he administered punishment.

I became a teacher of English. I made many mistakes–the chief one helped in the eventual writing of *Grammar Toward Professionalism*. I told my eighth grade class in a Friday moment of frustration, after having taught grammar for several weeks, that each student was to hand-write an essay on a subject of his or her choosing and if there were **any** mistakes that person would receive an automatic "F." Billy proudly handed in his paper on Monday. I graded it and I knew he had gotten the best of me and my ridiculous edict.

No sentence had more than four words. He had made no mistakes!
I have a kitten. Her name is Fluffy. I like Fluffy
I play with Fluffy. I feed Fluffy. *Ad nauseam.*
Billy was made to edit his paper using compound and compound-complex sentences. Again he taught me a great lesson. He wrote at the end of his rewritten copy, "I would be glad to correct the errors on my papers if I knew where to find the answers." Edison's light bulb turned on in my head! Mother had often said when we seven children couldn't find something, "If you put it where it belongs, then you can find it." Why not have them write **their** own grammar book under my direction and I will grade **their** papers

by giving them the page from **their** book which gives them the answer to the grammatical error on **their** composition? That was fifty–five years ago.

The McGuffey readers taught me much concerning multiple teaching. Why can't one teach mathematics while teaching grammar? Don't we use the same marks of punctuation for ratio as we do for colons? Doesn't "plus" in mathematics mean "and" in English? Why can't we teach science while teaching sentences models? Isn't a kangaroo a marsupial? Why can't we teach history while teaching appositives for comprehension? Abraham Lincoln, our sixteenth president, had much sorrow in his life. Why can't we teach positive leadership while teaching reading? What can you get from this actual happening that teaches you a valuable lesson?

Bobby was a born leader. He was sometimes a bit obnoxious to the adult observation but was an idol to his peers. Halloween, a shortened form of All Hallow Even, originated as an evening before All Saints Day when children would play harmless pranks on their elders. Bobby had no idea of the history behind the event but he and his cohorts learned a valuable lesson in evaluating whom you follow and who is fit to lead. Bobby and his group were going to ride their bicycles to the Cook farm about a mile into the country and isolated from humanity. They were going to put their bicycles behind the big blue Harvestore and gently creep to the front porch and slip a burned out match stick into the doorbell button causing it to ring continuously. They would run back to the secluded spot behind the silo where they would be able to see the frustration on their English teacher's face when she came to the door and found the ingenious invention protruding from the activated button. True leadership makes certain that the plan will work by surveying the necessary entities to make it work. They came to the farm. Only Bobby was brave enough to attempt the trip to the porch. He arrived to learn that his teacher had no doorbell! Why hadn't he thought of that? As he finished descending the five steps from the porch, Bobby forgot to turn off the flashlight. Around the corner of the house came the owner's huge canine, a mixture of gentleness obscured by size, and the dog gave a heart rending vocal version of a classroom's "listen up." Bobby's flashlight immediately conveyed "get out of here." He took off across the yard to get to the retreat behind the silo. His shortened exit route took him across the yard where a taunt close line awaited its next burden. Bobby caught this line across his forehead and the contact threw him and his flashlight first into the air and then to the ground. The flashlight's orbital circuit looked like fireworks which scared the dog. Bobby made his escape followed by his posse. The next day in English class while we were working on the book *Grammar Toward Professionalism*, I called on Bobby and mentioned this red line across his forehead. The class broke into simultaneous laughter and I wondered if I had fallen into a joke about which I knew nothing. The class couldn't wait to tell me about the great prank which had backfired because of leadership which had not done prior planning. Some of the model sentences in The Book were rewritten to incorporate this lesson to that class and to posterity. McGuffey knew what he was doing. Thank you Great Educator.

I taught grammar in high school for many years. There are other elements of teaching that need to be learned. One of them is listening closely to what is said. Study halls are the bane of every high school teacher. In fact, if an administration wants to get rid of a teacher, it gives him or her three study halls in place of classes. I had a study hall of seventy students the last period of the day in the cafeteria. Looking back, someone must have wanted to get rid of me and I was too naïve to notice. However, an experience which began there, prompted me to revise my book even further. Someone in the study hall was not only a ventriloquist but could also imitate bird calls masterfully. I could never "catch" the student until I was given another assignment which is also meant to prompt teachers to leave education. I had lunchroom duty in the gymnasium! The school had just purchased a trampoline which required spotters around it to prevent accidents. One of my "study hall" boys was trying it out and showing off by jumping too high. He went up and his blue jeans stayed on the trampoline. Someone called out, "Nice going, Birdman." Because I listened, I now knew the identity of my study hall "Birdman." Needless to say, listening is important. Much of my book involves the importance of listening.

High school seniors are different—especially toward the last three weeks of school when assignments need finalized. One of my favorite students and a star athlete decided that my assignment need not be done because he had it made—honor roll status, National Honor Society and B M O C (big man on court)athletically. He didn't hand in his research paper. He earned an "F" on his last six weeks grade in English. Later that young man became Director of the Football Hall of Fame in Canton, Ohio. He publicly attributed part of his success to an English teacher who taught him a lesson in completing one's duties even when statistically, "He had it made." He probably doesn't know this but he taught me a lesson when I, too, thought I had it made educationally and was tempted not to finish my assignment in the senior part of my life by not sharing my knowledge with those who may profit from it. I don't want to get an "F"; so here is my book. Dr. Martha J. B. Cook

All age groups can write history when they recall various segments of their lives and share them with others. The history you have just read has incidences from early age to career age. Take any segment and use it as an example for the group whose age it fits.

POETRY

Poetry is so versatile and flexible that it should be begun in the kindergarten. All the words to music are poetry; nearly all nursery rhymes are poetry. The most popular poetry is probably that which rhymes because it is easiest to memorize. However, poetry in prose may appeal to some because one does not have to be structured in words to fit a rhyme scheme. Poetry parallels best with music. The meter in poetry is similar to the beat in music. Some students learn their a,b,cs to music. Others learn the books of the Bible to music. Valentines are poetry; greeting cards are poetry. Parodying any of the above gives a personal touch to poetry which may make poetry more interesting later in life.

This poem was written by the author of this book when she was ask to assume the principalship of the school where she was counselor while the principal and assistant principal went to a conference. It was framed and given to the two men when they returned.

SHOES

On Thursday morn I wore with pride,
A pair of shoes by me untried.

On Friday with my feet inside,
You know, those darn shoes were too wide.

When Monday came, I laced them tighter,
Til noon I thought things seemed much brighter.

On Tuesday then, first thing I knew
Each step I took those same shoes grew.

Wednesday came and I walked a lot,
My feet came up; my shoes did not.

Once more Thursday rolled around,
The soles were thin; I felt the ground.

Friday dawned then as per pact
Thank God I gave those worn shoes back!

The moral in mixed metaphor,
Stems from the fact from old folklore.

If we the shoes of others wear
We'll find the grass no greener there.

Parodying a poem is fun; this is a favorite:

Some roses are white;
Some violets are too.
You are so bright
I really need you!

One of the poems most parodied is "The Night Before Christmas"—see what you can do with that one.

How about this one for the entire class to memorize no matter what age group?

You can't expect a boy (girl) like me
To stand up here where all can see
And make a speech as large as those
Who wear the finest kind of clothes.
Demosthenes and Cicero
Don't view me with a critic's eye
But pass all imperfections by.   Anonymous

It is always a good practice to memorize favorite lines from poetry if not the entire poem. Memorized lines may be used all one's life as quotes when appropriate.

Example:

You can lead a horse to water
But you cannot make him drink.

You can surround a fool with wisdom
But you cannot make him think.   Anonymous

Example from Robert Frost's "The Road Not Taken"

I shall be telling this with a sigh
Somewhere ages and ages hence:
Two roads diverged in a wood, and I—
I took the one less traveled by,
And that has made all the difference.

What tremendous bibliotherapeautic messages poems can give us in so few words!

Notice how most of these poems could be dramatized.